SOCIAL ISSUES, JUSTICE AND STATUS

THE MALTHUSIAN CENTURY

SOCIAL ISSUES, JUSTICE AND STATUS

Additional books in this series can be found on Nova's website under the Series tab.

Additional e-books in this series can be found on Nova's website under the e-book tab.

SOCIAL ISSUES, JUSTICE AND STATUS

THE MALTHUSIAN CENTURY

CHARLES T. STEWART, JR.

nova publishers
New York

For permission to use material from this book please contact us:
Telephone 631-231-7269; Fax 631-231-8175
Web Site: http://www.novapublishers.com

Library of Congress Cataloging-in-Publication Data

ISBN: 978-1-62948-667-3

Published by Nova Science Publishers, Inc. † New York

CONTENTS

PREFACE

Forecasts are for natural phenomena, which cannot react to invalidate them. There are realities in the future, to which current and future generations must adapt. What started as concern about economic problems and policy choices in the United States turned out to be shared by most of the rest of the world, which in addition faces pressure of population on resources that has not existed since the end of the ice age. Then it led to agriculture. I do not know the outcome this century, but consider some possible trajectories.

There are no footnotes, a few passing references. It is a work of speculation, not of scholarship. I owe much to dead and living sages, more to the diverse gang of octogenarians at the Starbucks on Sangamore Road, to Alan Greenberg, to Marvin Hass and his daily comments and references, and to the transatlantic exchange of ideas with Armand Braun in Paris.

Chapter 1

INTRODUCTION

The first edition of *An Essay on the Principle of Population* was published in 1798 in the early stages of the Industrial Revolution. Malthus foresaw world overpopulation but not when it would come to pass. No one could foresee the rates of growth of population or food supply or the time when the former would outstrip the latter. But given the fixed world supply of agricultural land and other resources, eventually there would not be enough food. War, disease, starvation would adjust population size to the supply of food. In fact population increased fairly slowly for the next century, from one billion in 1800 to 1.6 billion in 1900. Much of this growth was in Europe and North America.

Public health: sanitation, vaccination, but also better nutrition dramatically reduced infant, child, and maternal mortality in the late 19th and in the twentieth centuries. Agricultural productivity increased, providing better nutrition for the poor. World population took off, quadrupling in the 20th century.

If there are historians in the 25th century, they agree that the second millennium was characterized by three mega-historical events: first, the discovery of America, the export of the potato to Europe and maize and cassava to Africa and Asia; second, the scientific/industrial revolution; and third, the quadrupling of world population in the last century of the millennium. The result was the resource wars and other disasters early in the third millennium.

What no one foresaw was the dramatic decline in fertility rates in the second half of the 20th century, continuing today, which is beginning to reduce population in most advanced nations and slowing growth elsewhere. Great increases in productivity in agriculture and in other branches of production have allowed living levels to rise. So we need no longer be concerned with threat of starvation, disease, or war as means of limiting population?

Aspirations have changed, and so have circumstances. Mass starvation is no longer a threat except as a consequence of mistaken policies. Deadly epidemics are a remote threat, given our knowledge of medicine and public health. Only wars remain as a response to scarcity. But with higher incomes, scarcity is no longer focused on food but also on fuels, minerals. The Japanese invasions of the 1930s and 1940s were resource wars, but not in response to global scarcity. Japan sought the standard of living of Europe and North America, which it later achieved by other means.

The wars of the future will be competition for affluence, not for subsistence or survival. China and India today each have some ten times Japan's population, their growth in demand for resources is in excess of the world growth of supply. Prices will rise, increasing costs of living everywhere. Exhaustion of commercial supplies of coal, gas, petroleum is for some future century. This century we are consuming renewable resources in excess of their sustainable annual yield, not just ocean fisheries, but forests, and perhaps farmland. Their degradation reduces future yields. In this hemisphere the one example is Haiti, but China and a number of African nations are headed in that direction. The world cannot live beyond its means. The twentieth century is not sustainable. There are too many people, consuming too many resources, replenishable or not. The debt is due in the twenty first.

While aspirations have grown, prospects are bleak. The decline in fertility below replacement rate in most of the developed world and in much of the rest as well, notably China, means that the ratio of workers to population will be declining indefinitely. Increased longevity further contributes to this trend. Productivity must increase at a rate well above its past performance, or levels of living must decline. It is this conflict between the demand for affluence and declining fertility that is the 21st century version of the Malthusian vision, or nightmare. Malthus is still about overpopulation, but relative to resources, not just food, and about affluence, not just subsistence. The essays that follow all have some bearing on the prospects for affluence in the decades ahead. Most are future history, some are what ifs. The final essay elaborates on this introduction.

The twentieth century, was it the greatest of centuries? It was crowded with mega-historical events: two world wars, a world depression sandwiched in between; first men walking on the moon, robots roving over Martian soil, nuclear bombs and nuclear power; a quadrupling of world population combined with a large increase in affluence; near-doubling of the life span in advanced nations as public health, vaccines and antibiotics conquered infectious disease.

It was by far the most inventive century in history, as well as the century of discovery, in every field of inquiry. The number of scientists, engineers, scholars and masters of nearly all fields in this century probably exceeded the total in all previous history. Most world population became literate. Authority came under siege

The nineteenth was the age of steam and steel. The steam engine was a source of power in place, in factories, then railroads and steamships It was also the beginning of a new age of communication: the telegraph, and of manufacturing: interchangeable parts.

The twentieth was above all the day of electricity separating the source of power from its place of use, the universal source of power and light; of internal combustion engines, the motor vehicle, airplane, rocket; the telephone, radio, TV, and finally the computer everywhere, and the internet. It was the inventor of new materials, replacing the natural with the synthetic, the element with the compound, an escalation of complexity

What is left for the twenty first century? Characterized by new materials and machinery, or by intangibles: communication, information, surveillance, knowledge and adjustment to a decline in population and to increased longevity?

The essays that follow deal with the many and diverse issues that will concern us this century, the problems we must confront, and some of the policies that may be available. Each bears some relation to the fundamental concerns of the century, which are demographic. Since each is self-contained, some repetition is unavoidable and desirable. The final essay, "Farewell to Affluence", is future history attempting to impose some coherence on a diverse enterprise.

Chapter 2

THE INDUSTRIAL REVOLUTION IS OVER

The agricultural revolution lasted ten thousand years; the industrial. just two centuries. The icon of the industrial revolution was the Watt steam engine that initiated a rapid decline in the cost of energy. The 19th century was the age of steam, first energy in factories churning out large volumes at low costs; on rail and ship, cutting transportation time and cost, and the cost of everything to the final purchaser. In the first half of the 20th century, the internal combustion engine extended the transport revolution to small scale, short distances, and remote locations. The decline in transportation costs has been so large that it is not possible to have a similar decline in the future - transport cost cannot fall below zero.

Engines could only produce power in place. Electric power permitted large scale generation of power in a single location, and its distribution to wherever it was needed. Electrification transported energy everywhere to light the night, to replace manual labor at the level of the household. Electric power generation today, and the efficiency of machines and appliances using it, are vastly superior to what was available a century ago.

A second agricultural revolution that plummeted the cost of food and other products was made possible by the transportation revolution plus plant genetics, fertilizer, pesticides and herbicides and farm machinery. The Engel curve - the ratio of spending on food to total income - plunged. As in the case of transportation, it is impossible to achieve a decline in the cost of food in the future anywhere near as large as achieved in the past century and a half.

As to manufactured goods, the mix today is so different from what it was before the Industrial Revolution that a cost comparison is impossible. For textiles and apparel it is possible to say that the cost is a small fraction of what it was in 1776 and cannot decline a great deal in the future.

Perhaps the most important use of new sources of energy was transportation. Without the great reduction in transport cost via train, steamer, truck, the gains from manufacturing would have been much smaller. Transportation cost may be difficult to compare across centuries, but time is an unchanging variable. The stagecoach trip from Washington to New York took a week. Today Amtrak does it in 3 hours without need for meals, overnight accommodations, or loss of several days of work. Costs as well as time per ton/mile of freight transport are also a small fraction of what they once were.

Energy itself may no longer be declining in cost. Today the drive is on to replace hydrocarbon fuels with carbon-free and with renewable sources of energy. We are a long way from solar energy competitive with coal or natural gas and may never get there.

The agricultural revolution exploited renewable resources. There were few people on the planet. They spent much of their income, or labor, on food, basic clothing, shelter and war. The Industrial revolution was based on depletable resources, coal and petroleum prominent among them. The population explosion that followed greatly accelerated the rate of exploitation of nonrenewable resources of all kinds, fuels among them. Sooner or later the resort to poorer or less accessible supplies is bound to raise costs.

PRODUCTIVITY SLOWDOWN?

The next technological revolution was in communication, anticipated by the telegraph, actualized by radio, telephone, and more recently by TV and the Internet. These were more improvements in the quality of life than declines in cost of living. They are not just better, cheaper ways of producing the same old thing, but also products - services - qualitatively different from anything we had before.

In the second half of the twentieth century the revolution in communications evolved piggy back into the current information revolution. But we no longer see the payoff in levels of living experienced in the 19th and early 20th centuries. The real earnings of a full time full year worker were unchanged for the past half century. Incomes rose because of a large increase in the ratio of workers to population: 58% in 1960, reaching 67% in the past decade, now 64%. We owe it to the increased labor force participation of women..

Each trajectory has its limits. We can build cars with 800 horsepower that go 200mph, but where can they go, and what for at high cost? We could propel passengers from one city to another in a fraction of the time it takes today, at huge cost, and who could stand the acceleration? Our demand for food is limited; below some low price, further reductions become of trivial importance in our budgets. If our taste for clothing is not so limited, cheaper clothing requires a larger more expensive house to store it.

Looking at technological change since 1776, it appears that it increased real incomes dramatically, but that it is no longer doing so. The great inventions of the past: steam engine, internal combustion engine, electric power, and their major applications in production and transportation multiplied productivity, elevated our levels of living. Technology of recent decades in communication, information, entertainment has contributed a great deal to our life styles, but little to our living levels. We have not repealed the law of diminishing returns.

Computers and information technology were doomed to have smaller economic impact than their predecessor major inventions because they came late, after so much had been accomplished in reducing costs and increasing incomes. From the viewpoint of impact on costs and income, the limit is zero. Infinite speed, infinite capacity, infinite precision are technological, not economic goals. In fact the impact of computers, electronics and information technology has been huge, but much of it is on the productivity of the household and on quality of life Think of TVs, microwave ovens, computers, portable phones. The household economy is not included in national income and product accounts. The equipment and its operating costs must be paid by income earned in the market economy. At this time we don't know the extent of recent gains in productivity. Available data have a strong upward bias and need revision. They assume a closed economy. But with free trade and cheap transport, there has been a strong outsourcing trend in manufacturing and to some extent in services. When a firm outsources part of its supply chain or production process, cost declines are registered as productivity increases in the United States, although the lower costs may be in Taiwan or China. A second source of upward bias in productivity measures is product improvement reflected in higher value of output. But insofar as it increases productivity, it is for the buyer, not the producer.

WHAT IS LEFT?

What is left to contribute the large productivity gains that in the past drove up per capita income and the share of income disposable, to purchase new, better products and services? We cannot expect the big gains in cost of food and other farm products, in manufactured goods, in transportation time and cost, communications cost, speed, volume.

What is left that has not experienced the gains in productivity are services, in particular education and health care. That is why they are a large and growing share of the economy. Is there much scope for productivity gain in either? The biggest industry is health care, absorbing 18% of the GDP, predicted to grow as more people are covered by health insurance, and keep on rising until the baby boom generation passes on. Without severe cost-cutting there is no prospect of any increase in disposable income in the foreseeable future, and every likelihood of a decline. Prices and earnings are too high, partly the result of deliberate restriction of supply, partly attributable to lawyers. This is a distributional issue. There are also issues of excessive care, low productivity, and inefficient organization.

How can one question the productivity of health care? Early in the past century, public health: safe water, milk, and vaccines reduced infant mortality from 100 to 8 per thousand. It reduced the cost of rearing a child to working age. More recently, largely as a result of antibiotics, there has been a large increase in life expectancy among the elderly. Since most of them are not working and earning, it could actually reduce per capita income.

It is improved health among working age adults that matters. Humans are diverse in their response to disease and medication. Individualized health care is one direction of research. We cannot predict the balance of costs and benefits. Most of the time we have no better decision process than trial and error, but not for long. Yet given the current health status of workers, we cannot expect much or indefinitely continuing gain from improved health care. Without major breakthroughs in technology and mores, health improvements are counter-productive. They simply prolong the lives of those who do not and usually cannot work, increasing the dependency ratio, diverting resources from more productive uses, lowering income per capita. The health advances which paid off in economic terms were made long ago, public health, vaccination, penicillin, reducing infant and child mortality, improving the health of children and working age adults

Education is around 7.6 % of GDP, not counting household expenditures other than payments to schools. These include educational materials and equipment, private tutors and teachers, including home schooling. It has grown because there is more to learn than in the past, greater need to know, but also because we have more money to spend. On productivity we know from comparisons over time that we did better a hundred years ago than in the present. But beyond elementary school it was for a smaller and more select proportion of the population. From international comparisons we know that other countries also with universal education do a good deal better than we do.

As to college education, there is a question of objectives, the issue of who decides, who teaches, who enrolls. Only for given objectives is it possible to make comparisons over time or internationally. Are we trading off productivity for numbers in excess of those needed for the economy? Are we focusing on objectives unrelated to economic performance?

From the viewpoint of labor force productivity it is not clear that there was any improvement since the GI Bill of Rights equalized opportunity for college education. The disappearance of vocational training in high schools is a decline in productivity. The huge increase in college enrollments postpones labor force entry by years. It does not reflect the needs and opportunities of the economy, inasmuch as the specializations that contribute most to productivity advance have declined as a share of graduates. I refer to scientific and technological majors, who will conduct research and contribute most of the inventions that advance productivity and generate new products and services. We are highly dependent on immigrants for work and for instruction in science and technology. A near-quadrupling of the share of the labor force with a college degree in the past half century has not led to a surge of productivity and economic growth.

But how does better education or better health translate into productivity per worker? Given the high cost of some productivity-enhancing educational and health policies, are they worth the cost? These are not questions we need to raise with respect to the steam engine, the electric light. For them the market is the test.

Gains in human learning, health, and competence are not comparable with the big gains in mass production. In a factory, old machines are replaced with much more efficient new machines; in education it is always the same human being that must be educated. Ultimately there are limits to human memory, processing capabilities and speed, creativity. Possibilities are a function of advances in knowledge. New technology will reduce the monetary costs of learning, but not the time and effort costs. The best prospects appear to be individualized learning - instruction based on advances in cognitive science.

Progress in education and health is constrained by the genetic code. There is no such barrier to technology. It is as though progress were limited to improving the performance of James Watt's original steam engine, no new models.

Throughout human history, military technology has been an important component of invention, often leading to major civilian applications. This past century the airplane, radar, computers, the Internet were developed for military use. The military are achieving great economies via replacement of manned bombers and fighters, extremely costly to manufacture and to operate, with unmanned aircraft. Such craft, as well as guided missiles, doom the fabulously expensive aircraft carrier, which will soon follow the battleship into oblivion. But this is a small percentage of GDP. Some of the same technologies, robotic - will economize somewhat on the cost of production of goods and services. NASA's requirements for new materials, for efficient energy supply, are another source of potential productivity gains in the economy at large. But this borders on science fiction, not a prescription for prosperity

Short of a scientific breakthrough offering unlimited amounts of energy at close to zero costs - the perpetual dream of nuclear fusion energy - there seems no prospect of sustained growth rates in the future, of any increase in per capita income for any advanced nation (short of a resource bonanza, such as Norway's North Sea oil).

These pessimistic conclusions do not take into account the demographic revolution ongoing in nearly all the world: dramatic declines in fertility rates, with subsequent declines in the ratio of workers to population. lowering per capita income for any given level of labor productivity. We just don't know how this demographic transition will work out, nor how long before returning to some stable pattern.

PROGRESS IN THE FUTURE?

Today we face the end of upward mobility. It is one implication of declining incomes. What shall we do about the idea of progress? We have defined progress in terms of levels of living. We have defined upward mobility in terms of occupation and income. There can be no net upward mobility if there is no gain in income even if there should be some upgrading of occupational structure. But progress can be viewed from other perspectives. In America progress first took the form of a moving frontier. That is now closed. But ours is still a frontier nation mentality. There are frontiers other than those defined by geography.

Underlying the idea of progress is the idea of continuous change. What change we consider to be progress is a question of culture. The United States derives its identity not from ethnicity or history, but from its ideology. It is the one ideological nation in world history. We have learned to view progress in terms of personal freedom, equality of opportunity, democratic government, as well as rising personal incomes. Since the end of the First World War the nation has labored to expand its ideological frontiers, making the world safe for democracy, its leadership in the post-world war II era in defending the free world, and on a different level, its going concern about human rights, both at home and abroad. Can these concerns replace the traditional focus on economic progress? The scientific revolution is not just about productivity but about knowledge. The pursuit of happiness need not be the standard of living; it must become the quality of life and liberty.

Chapter 3

ALTERNATIVE ENERGY: GEOGRAPHY AND ARITHMETIC

Concern about the fuel we burn has a long history. At first it was about coal and the plumes of soot, sulfur and other particulates from its burning. It was about health and the great London fogs. Then the public became aware of the sulfur, acid rain and its environmental impact. With the oil crises of 1973 and 1979 attention turned to petroleum supply and cost, and our dependence on imports. Only recently has attention shifted to the emission of carbon dioxide and its effect on climate, whatever the hydrocarbon fuel concerned.

The early concerns have not been forgotten; to some extent they have been addressed. We are less dependent on petroleum imports than we were. n Canada and Mexico, our major suppliers, are not the same thing as the Middle East. Any time we want to increase our domestic oil production, we know exactly where to drill and how. Ethanol is the only policy that directly addresses the issue of self-sufficiency in oil. Fuel efficiency standards also help. Much has been done to clean up emissions, whether power plants or motor vehicles. It is carbon dioxide emissions and their impact on climate that now dominate alternative energy policies.

The term "alternative energy" usually implies renewable energy, natural forces, primarily wind and sunlight, that produce no emissions, but it often includes emission-producing fuels. organic materials that are burned but are renewable: agricultural waste, wood. Renewable itself refers to two separate concerns. One is a very long term perspective, a fear of a remote future in which fossil fuels: coal, oil, natural gas, will be depleted, exhausted or prohibitively expensive. The other, more immediate, is the fear of global climate change and the contribution of hydrocarbon fuels to that change.

More or less forgotten is the older concern about air pollution in terms of health rather than climate. It has nothing to do with global warming, since the particulate emissions from burning coal contribute to cooling. The biggest recent contribution toward global cooling was the massive eruption of Mt. Pinatubo in the Philippines in 1991.

There is not much to be said in behalf of organic alternatives.. Ethanol from corn is an epic disaster, costly, diverting large areas of farmland from food production, driving up food prices, and doing little to reduce consumption of petroleum. Ethanol from sugar cane is much more efficient, competitive with oil, with a large current and larger potential output, but not in the United States. It also is a diversion of fertile land from other valuable uses. As to agricultural waste, it is expensive to collect, has alternative value in preserving the soil, and has a limited potential supply. Hydropower is fully used, perhaps overused, as some dams are being destroyed, some reservoirs are silting up.

Wind power produces no emissions. Its advantage over solar energy is that it is available at night as well as day, from the equator to the pole. At this time it is also cheaper than solar. Its great disadvantage is lack of continuity or periodicity. Most of our wind energy capacity is idle most of the time, and its transmission network also. Storage requirements for practical use would be enormous. But in a country of this size the wind is blowing somewhere all the time. Access of wind farms to transmission networks nationwide is an alternative to unavailable storage. But it does mean enormous wind farms throughout the nation, a vast overcapacity. The tradeoff between storage and transmission, with overcapacity at both ends, is not arithmetic, it is math. But wind unpredictability is such that transmission seems to be the better option. Either option would escalate the cost of what is already an expensive source of energy.

Wind power is low density, in terms of kilowatts per square mile. Wind farms demand space. I know of no estimates of the current area committed to them, but there are estimates of kilowatt hours generated per square mile, and current capacity. Assuming 25% efficiency, 500kw per square mile, in 2012 the total area occupied by wind turbines was some 4,200 square miles, or a square 65 miles on each side. This area is almost twice the land area of Delaware, almost as large as Connecticut. This capacity was contributing just under 4% of total electric power. The goal of 20% would mean multiplying this area more than 5 times, spread in the windiest areas. There could be a massacre of the bird population. As the area expands, it tends to move into less wind power-efficient areas. The cheapest lands are near the arctic ocean and in national parks.

It is solar energy that is the future of energy, but not the future forever. It is ubiquitous, inexhaustible, and high density. Unlike wind, it is periodic; length of day and night are precisely predictable. Sunlight during any one day cannot be predicted, perhaps not even a week ahead, but over a month or year it can be estimated fairly closely. This means we can calculate capacity requirements and storage needs.

The day is roughly 12 hours long at the equator. The farther away from the equator, the greater the variation in the length of day. June 21 in Seattle is 16 hours long; December 21 only 8. This means that twice the solar cell capacity is needed to provide the same amount of energy in December as in June. Excess capacity the rest of the year, and costs, increase as one moves away from the equator. Furthermore, at the equator, the sun at noon is directly overhead twice a year, and close the rest of the year. Far from the equator, the sun at noon is closer to the horizon, its rays at an acute angle, penetrating far more atmosphere than at the equator.

But energy needs are not 8 hours a day in December; they are 24 hours, wherever you live. Hence the need for storage if energy supply is to be solar. The farther away from the equator, the greater the overnight storage capacity required. Solar energy is best designed for the tropics, where inter-seasonal differences in needs are minimal. As in the case of wind, the tradeoff between storage and transmission is a complex calculus, but much easier, since sunlight is much more predictable than wind.

Since the continental US has only 3 time zones, there is little scope for transporting solar energy between east and west when one coast is in daylight while the other is at night. For overnight needs, the solution is storage. But Eurasia encompasses 12 time zones between Ireland and the Bering Strait, its geography offers the prospect of substituting energy transmission between time zones. Nationalism is an obstacle.

The farther from the equator the greater the disparity in sunlight between summer and winter. The local alternative of excess capacity and months-long storage is not available. Storage of vast amounts of solar energy for several months is for some future century. The potential alternative is north-south inter-hemispheric transmission. The western Hemisphere is continuous from Artic Ocean to Patagonia. For Eurasia, the only route from Arctic to Antarctic is to South Africa, nothing further south. For inter-seasonal disparities in supply, the answer must be transmission.

The capacity for large scale overnight storage does not exist, nor for inter-seasonal storage. The technology that would make them possible at less than exorbitant cost does not exist. Overnight storage is at least conceivable; inter-seasonal is speculative science fiction; so is overnight long distance high capacity transmission.

Until such time as the storage technology is developed and the capacity generated, most of our energy, in the neighborhood of 80%, must come from sources that can produce on demand at any time of day or year. These are hydrocarbon (mainly coal and natural gas) and nuclear. No matter how much wind and solar capacity is installed, there are many times when there is no sun, no wind. The capacity needs for base power will not decline. What will decline is the efficiency of base power, as surplus wind or solar is introduced into the grid intermittently and unpredictably.

One should not forget that the Industrial Revolution was fundamentally a dramatic decline in the cost of energy: the steam engine. This decline has continued to the present, propelled by new technology and fuels. Electricity delivers cheap energy to anyone almost anywhere. The cost of energy is the basic determinant of our levels of living. Efforts to reverse this process by raising energy costs reduce real incomes. The public should be informed

Masochism at the national level is beyond my understanding. Why insist on doing what is possible to raise the cost of energy when a much more effective way of reducing carbon dioxide emissions by a much larger amount is available, which would lower the cost of energy, increasing our incomes? I refer to natural gas, much cleaner than coal, and currently a good deal cheaper. Germany, which proposes to abandon nuclear energy and derive 80% of its energy needs from renewable resources, may become the first nation to be hospitalized by a collision with reality. Subsidizing investment in inefficient technologies is not the way to promote research but to encourage rent-seeking. Far better to subsidize research directly.

Chapter 4

CLIMATE CHANGE AND COMMON SENSE

The first principle of change is that there are always both winners and losers. The big gainers from continued global warming are Canada and Russia. Think of amber fields of grain from Bering Strait to Labrador, from Murmansk to Kamchatka. The U.S would be a small gainer; Alaska is one fifth of its area, and Montana, Idaho, the Dakotas, Minnesota, Wyoming another very large chunk. Canada could become a nation of over 100 million people, with large cities in the Yukon Territory and Baffin Island. Russia would worry about which countries were sending workers and settlers to its vast Siberian farmlands.

Any review of climate history during human residence on earth will reveal that climate determinants beyond human influence or even knowledge are many times as important as human; that the current climate regime of 12,000 years is unique in its stability that some large natural change is overdue, and we will have to adjust. During the 200,000 years in which humans have lived on earth, ocean levels have varied by 100 meters, not the inches we are concerned about today. Fifty thousand years ago humans walked from the Asian mainland almost all the way to Australia. Only a short bamboo raft paddle was needed from New Guinea. Eight thousand years ago a rising Mediterranean overflowed, creating the Black Sea. Human activity had nothing to do with this huge range of climate.

The hysterical climate masters do not recognize how small is the role of human activity in the total dynamics of climate change, how limited their influence. We know about El Nino, La Nina, the 11-year sunspot cycle. They are small, short term. But changes in earth orbit have much greater and longer lasting influence on climate. We can predict them, when inner planets are between us and the sun, or outer planets lined up behind us. There are long term fluctuations in solar radiation and changes in earth's molten core, which we cannot predict. Our only possible response is adaptation.

Today we cannot measure the contribution of humans to climate warming (or change). Climate models do not predict the history of the twentieth century, or what happened in the past 15 years. There are too many missing variables and interactions, and no doubt some errors in measurement. But that does not justify inertia; models will improve.

What are left, subject to our influence, are really small potatoes. In addressing them we should first distinguish between causes and consequences. The frequent charge that it is the industrial revolution, replacing renewable materials with coal and iron, is nonsense. Burning wood produces more emissions per kilowatt hour than coal. If 7 billion people were burning and building with wood, there would be no trees left on the planet by now. Renewable does not mean renewed.

The cause is not coal, but people. Carbon dioxide is a diversion, recent increase a product of population growth and affluence, the real culprits. Population grew 60% during the 19th century, but quadrupled during the 20th. Even worse, it grew in affluence. Thus output grew between five and six fold. With world population still rising, the world-wide quest for affluence seems doomed. Income per capita in the developed world is already falling. It is the Malthusian century, not starvation or disease, perhaps warfare, but surely the moral death of diminished expectations. There is no consideration of optimum population. That is just as well, since we lack the policies to achieve it, or hope of agreeing on its international distribution.

Emissions from hydrocarbon fuels, renewable or not, are not good for us, warming or no warming, and should be reduced and eventually eliminated. What can be done? Efficiency in the use of energy and materials is always a good policy, but it will not take us very far very fast. Research to increase the efficiency of solar panels is a priority, to bring down the cost closer to that of coal and gas. Storage of one day's sunshine for overnight, perhaps next day's use at reasonable cost is another possible research aim. It would increase the share of solar in total energy consumption. But storage of summer sunshine for winter use is science fiction.

Population will be declining in nearly all affluent nations, but how long will this decline continue, how far will it go? It is their basic resource. Which nations are willing to scale back their efforts to achieve affluence? Which affluent nations are willing to consider substantial declines in their level of living? These questions refer to the losers from global warming. As to the gainers, they would be out of their minds to bear any of the costs of reducing climate change.

We have not agreed upon, or even discussed, the issue of optimum climate. We have not even considered the criteria to be used. The lesson from our current concern is that the optimum is always yesterday's.

The assumption that the sum of gains and losses from climate change will be negative and large is unsupported. The assumption that the benefits of human action to reduce climate warming are greater than their costs has no empirical basis and (therefore) is never discussed. I suspect that the benefit/cost ratio, and the impact on temperature, of current American efforts is approximately zero. Any gain will accrue predominantly to the rest of the world, not to the benefactor, whereas the cost will be borne exclusively by the benefactor.

The advantage of adaptation to change versus obstruction of change is that adaptation is local, national, whereas obstruction must be global. Climate today is warmer that the average for the past century, but not as warm as it has been more than once during human residence on earth. Human civilization flourished in both cold and warm periods. These are facts. Then there is grandiose faith in the ability of humans to shape climate and the absurd belief in the willingness of winners and losers to agree on goals and cooperate in the climate-shaping enterprise. The very idea that we can manipulate climate is Olympian presumption. I call it the Canute Complex. King Canute sat on the beach and ordered the rising tide to recede. He wet his pants. I am for efficiency, but not for self-immolation. Find another faith.

Why should European governments, and now our own, be so self-victimizing on energy-environment policy, taxing productive activities to subsidize inefficient alternatives such as solar energy? There is no prospect that solar will be competitive any time soon, since the capacity of an intermittent energy supplier must be a large multiple of that of coal or gas to generate the same amount of energy.

Obsession with carbon dioxide emissions is smokestack vision. There are other sources of warming subject to some human control. Deforestation may be the most important. Burning sequestered carbon releases huge amounts of carbon dioxide into the atmosphere. The rate of sequestration is reduced. The change in albedo contributes to warming, so does the reduction in evapotranspiration. But the main perpetrators are Indonesia and Brazil. Much of sub-Saharan Africa is at risk, as are the South American nations ringing the Amazon basin.

To understand current attitudes one must distinguish between the motivation of business and that of religion. Business is about making a living, about profit and loss. In the public sector, it is about benefit and cost; the cost/benefit ratio is equivalent to the profit and loss of business. In religion one does not ask, what is the profit from good behavior, is morality a good investment? One does not do cost-benefit analysis of the Ten Commandments. In religion, virtue is its own reward; if there are practical gains, so much the better, but such gains or losses are not determinants of behavior. They do not enter into moral accounting, and usually cannot be measured.

Environmentalism can be either business or religion. The trouble with the global warming religion denomination is that it worships false gods. Warming is Evil, and Carbon dioxide is its Agent, the Devil if you wish, and the Good, God is the absence of Evil, no carbon dioxide emissions, no warming, perhaps the Status Quo Ante.

Some 80% of power must be hydrocarbon or nuclear in most nations, no matter how much intermittent energy is generated. No city can store one day's sunlight for another day, never mind a month or two of summer sunlight for the winter months. Storage would simply increase the cost. Switching from coal to gas will accomplish more than an infinite number of windmills and solar panels in reducing emissions, and lower the cost of energy as well. Research should focus on cheap overnight storage; research, not investment.

Chapter 5

ECOPHILIA

Green means environmentalist, it also means neophyte. There are econuts, ecofanatics, and thoughtful caretakers, reasonable individuals concerned about the environment. How does one classify different shades of Greens? Green is not a primary color, just a mix of blue for depression and yellow for warning. The main distinction is between those who look back and those who look forward.

First and always there is eco-nostalgia. Let us if possible restore the countryside, the environment to its status quo ante. Supporters will disagree on the status ante to which the environment is to be restored, and what aspects of the environment are to be restored. Among them we should include those who seek to avoid changes in the environment, who therefore wish to preserve it as it is, or as it was quite recently. Efforts to prevent the extinction in the wild of the American eagle, the Florida alligator, many other species go back to the beginning of the century. But in restoring the landscape - the forests and waterways, they seek more than preservation, they seek the reversal of trends of the past two centuries in this country, much longer in other nations.

How much land should be reforested, how much of the original prairie restored? Should the Everglades be returned to its original state and area? If only the land could thunder to the hooves of buffalo or brontosaurus! The implicit assumption is that there are far too many people, that population should be reduced, urbanization reversed, industry greatly diminished.

Some eco-nostalgia is quaint and harmless; some has considerable aesthetic value; and some is plain nutty, such as the efforts to dis-employ thousands and resettle tens of thousands, to abandon flood control, irrigation, power generation to preserve some sub-sub species of guppy recently discovered if not invented whose habitat is disturbed, or some local subspecies of spotted owl abundant elsewhere. There are other habitats, we don't need every indistinguishable sub-sub species, evolution has created many, destroyed many, and we cannot stop its course. Nostalgia has its place, but it cannot recreate the past.

Other environmental activists are not concerned with going back to the past, or even with stopping the clock for its own sake, but with the viability of the total environment for future generations. Among the futurists, as with nostalgia, there may be disagreement on which status post is the cause of concern; which generation, which century, or is it millennium? It is not the loss of forests, but consequent changes in climate, decline in soil productivity. It is not air and water pollution, but harm to health. It is not dams and reservoirs disturbing natural environment (and human populations) but long term salinization resulting from irrigation, loss of breeding areas for important fish populations. It is the future decline in living standards resulting from wasteful exhaustion of various natural resources.

Of course, sensible environmental conservation coexists with fanaticism. As in the case of nostalgia, the implicit culprit is the growth of population, of industry and income. But there is a potential savior: new technology. Thus CFCs will be eliminated. Hydrocarbon fuels could be replaced with renewable sources of energy which do not pollute the air. The problem with technological salvation is that it is also the curse that has permitted enormous growth in population and food supply, the combustion of ever larger amounts of hydrocarbons per capita.

The Eco futurists are not of one method. There are those who focus on a problem and seek solutions. And there are others who peddle solutions and create problems. What distinguishes the latter is their reversal of the relation between research, invention, and investment. In the normal course of progress toward an objective one considers alternative approaches, conducts research and feasibility studies, then reaches a decision and takes the leap toward investment in the chosen solution. Investment is by far the most costly step in this sequence, one dares not take it blindfolded. But there are some futurists who think they know the answer, and are impatient for results.

They promote high cost investment in the expectation that research results will follow and costs fall. They commit resources to technologies they hope to render obsolete. But by subsidizing investment that cannot pass a market test, then subsidizing inefficient production, they reduce funding for research if not incentives. Premature investment becomes a vested interest diverting resources from investment in better technologies. Somehow this perverse sequence has gained the upper hand in several European nations, which are learning that they cannot afford it. It was money and time down the drain. In this nation, corn ethanol has been a disaster for fuel costs and food prices, and the electric car is a continuing liability. far more costly than and as polluting as the cars it is intended to replace. Fortunately Americans are not buying.

The fundamental variable in nostalgia for the past and fears for the future is population. The world is overpopulated. What is the optimum population, how determined, how attained? On this not one word. Meanwhile fertility rates have fallen below replacement level in much of the world, and are declining everywhere else, fewer carbon dioxide-exhaling bipeds in our future to spoil the environment.

The crusade of the future is population. What should be the global limit on bipeds? How many should each nation be allowed to have? Should international migration be restricted?

Chapter 6

A PLACE TO LIVE

We have been told that it is stupid to pay rent year after year, and at the end of the day have nothing to show for it. It is better to buy. Before the 2008 recession two thirds of households followed that advice. Since then most of them have experienced a significant decline in the market value of their home, some to below the inflation adjusted purchase price, a few to less than their mortgage debt. How long will it take to recover their losses, how much will they recover, and will their investment ever pay off? The answers are respectively, slowly, not much, and for most, no.

HOUSING CRISIS, HOUSING SLUMP

A mortgage is a long term commitment by both borrower and lender. At one time lenders required a substantial down payment and considered the borrower's income in terms of ability to keep up mortgage payments. They thought long term, protecting potential borrowers from unsustainable debt. More recently the basic assumption has been that housing prices would keep rising. Hence a mortgage with little down payment to a borrower of low and uncertain income was not high risk. Should the borrower default, the sales price of the foreclosed home would exceed the amount of mortgage owed. Besides, it was public policy to make such loans.

Banks knew that rising prices were not forever. They understood that if too many houses were foreclosed and placed on the market, prices would fall. But they did not know when. No bank had any incentive to refrain from lending in order to prevent such an outcome. It was a classic case of the common fallacy of composition. Unintended consequences followed. The residential loan default rate, under 2% through 2006, escalated to 11% in 2010, still in the 10% range in 2013. The foreclosure rate, less than 1% through 2007, jumped to 3% in 2009, to nearly 4% in the two subsequent years, still an estimated 3.4% for 2013. Home prices dropped. The continued high rate of defaults despite the successive years of foreclosures indicates that foreclosures will remain high in the next few years.

New construction dropped to less than a third of its 2006 peak, with little recovery since. This decline drove up the unemployment rate. It also more than compensated for the overexpansion in previous years, driving vacancy rates back down. The continuing low rate of new construction is now more an effect of unemployment and low incomes than a cause. The extraordinary decline in labor force participation, from 66.2 in 2007 to 63.2.% so far in 2013 is without precedent, a new concern. It is problematic at a time when working age population will be declining as a share of total population.

A second housing slump is about to start, this one is shallow, slow moving, long lasting. Home buying by baby boomers is about over, house selling just starting as they begin to retire. The baby boom generation was nearly twice as large as its predecessor, and more affluent. Thus its demand for housing was much larger than that of the generation of the Great Depression. This pattern of each generation being larger than its predecessor had prevailed in the past; the future will be different. Each successor generation so far is somewhat smaller than its predecessor, hence demand for housing should trend down, and construction employment likewise.

As baby boomers sell to their successors, the supply of housing for sale will tend to exceed the demand, depressing prices. This depression will not persist, as the housing industry will adjust by reducing construction, but it does mean that another major sector of the economy faces stagnation or decline.

Once the boomer generation is gone, much depends on the fertility rates of successive generations. Assuming they continue somewhat below replacement rates, population growth would slow down or end. There would be a slow decline in the rate of new construction, a decline in employment.

Fertility is not the only determinant of future needs for housing, Net international migration has boosted demand in the past, more than we expect it to do in the future.. Much demand for new housing in recent decades has been a move to the suburbs, abandonment of central city residential areas. The rising cost of land and the ubiquity of cars made their departure necessary and possible. This is over, reducing the need for new housing, As to shifts of employment between cities, who can predict their magnitude in the decades ahead?

Is home ownership a good investment? It depends on when the purchase was made, since prices change over time, and so do interest rates on mortgages. 2009 and 2010 were good years to buy foreclosed houses, if you could get a mortgage. The previous decade was not. It also depends on location.

WHERE TO LIVE

Last century America completed a process of urbanization plus suburbanization. Many farms, villages, small towns disappeared. Despite a quadrupling of population, even some large cities lost much of their population, starting with Pittsburgh, since recovered, and currently Detroit. Imagine what happened to home values in that city. This century, with much slower population growth, urban population decline will be the fate of many more cities than in the past.

Suburbanization was a search for cheap housing. But it was also an epidemic of nostalgia for a more self-sufficient life style, also much more laborious. Why should houses still be built with fireplace and chimney?

Why live far out for a lilac bush, tomato and dandelion garden, or monotonous green grass that convention requires mowing? The ideal urban garden is a flower pot, which can be brought indoors in winter, providing a flower garden year-round in any clime. But there is nostalgia even in city centers. Trees grow on top of New York high rises. Soil is treasured.

Suburbs were havens for families with children. But children grow up and leave, parents age. Housing needs change over a lifetime. There are fewer children today, far more elderly living alone. Half the households with head 75 years of age and older are single-person, their number is likely to double. Detached homes in suburbs are no place for single person households.

From a social rather than individual perspective, suburbs demand far more miles of pipe, wire, cement and asphalt, bus lines, car commuting per household, not to mention all the time required from origin to many frequent destinations. There are economies of scale and scope in cities as there are in large residential buildings.

Apartments make sense for single person, single parent households. Living in apartment buildings, condominiums, coops sacrifices some property rights. Are dogs allowed, may I play the piano at night? But they offer economies of scale, central heating and air conditioning, laundry, security, convenient maintenance and repair services, social and entertainment facilities.

They are time savers for single parent households. No one should live alone in a detached house in the suburbs.

We can expect a rapid growth in the number of elderly who can no longer live alone, but cannot afford assisted living or nursing homes. They and their family will have to decide how to cope, whether by depletion of assets and disinheritance in order to qualify for Medicaid, or by other means which would increase average household size instead of diminishing it. These choices will influence the type of residence to be built.

We cannot predict 20 or 30 years in advance what will happen to residential values in particular areas within large cities, nor which cities will experience large losses of basic economic activity and population The information and communication revolution will have consequences, as did nearly universal car ownership. This uncertainty is the futurist's case for renting versus owning. A city with varied economic base is safer than one with a single dominant industry, but many workers have no choice of cities.

RENTING VS. OWNING

Memories of what happened in recent years to the value of housing, defaults and foreclosures, will linger. Ownership doesn't seem to be as good an investment as it was once considered. Expectations of rising incomes are unlikely to survive the recession.

Banks have been burned by bad loans. They will require significant down payments and scrutinize the borrower's ability to make the mortgage payments in terms of income, employment stability and credit record. Many would-be owners, who could have easily obtained mortgage loans in the past, will not be able to borrow in the foreseeable future. As to down payments, Americans today save much less than they did 50 years ago, when their incomes were lower, 2% (higher in recession) versus up to 10% then. Owners who have been foreclosed will not be entitled to borrow for quite a few years.

Banks have been burned by bad loans. They will require significant down payments and/or scrutinize the 'would be' borrower's ability to meet the terms of the mortgage in terms of income, employment stability and credit record. Many would-be owners, who could have easily obtained mortgage loans in the past, will not be able to borrow in the foreseeable future. As to down payments, Americans today save much less than they did 50 years ago, when their incomes were somewhat lower, 2% (higher in recession years) versus up to 10% then. Owners who have been foreclosed will not be entitled to borrow for quite a few years.

The federal income tax itemized deduction for interest payments on mortgages should be abolished and probably will be. It is an indirect subsidy for lenders and builders, direct for affluent home buyers paid in part by taxpayers who cannot afford to buy a home. Besides, it is an attempt to promote immobility in a mobile society and economy. It is renting that makes sense in such a society for most people.

The risks of loss of value of residential property are higher than they were in the 20th century. Population will not be growing much, and will be more likely to decline in a larger number of cities. The proportion of households owning their homes has been too high. It is falling and will continue falling for some time, by necessity and by choice.

. Renting is a means of shifting such long term risks to those who own homes as a business, not as a place to live: to landlords. Call it insurance.

Chapter 7

SAVINGS, INVESTMENT AND SALVATION

The story of America can be written in terms of key inventions: barbed wire, cotton gin, electric light, car, computer. But progress is a joint enterprise. Investment in plant, equipment, human skills bring inventions to society, and savers finance both invention and investment.

Business is still saving, but household saving has tanked. One would expect national personal saving to rise with income, as it does for individuals, but it was much higher when the nation was poorer. Personal saving in the 1960s was in the 8-9% annual rate; For the 1970's, it was somewhat higher, from 8% to nearly 11%. During the 1980s the 8 to 10% range held until 1986, when it began a decline to 6%. The 1990s were in the 5-7% range, but starting in 2000 the rate dropped to 2% and remained in the 2-3% range until 2008, when it rose to 5%, where it remains today. Savings rates rise in periods of uncertainty.

People save as a precaution for an uncertain future. The most important motivation has been for retirement. People also save for specific goals: to buy a home and today, to finance a college education. What has changed to drive down savings so low so fast?

PUBLIC POLICIES

Public policies, and more recently, business practices, have undermined the motivation to save. The introduction of Social Security in 1935 weakened the motivation to provide for old age. In 1964, Medicare guaranteed some reimbursement for health care for retirees. Both were financed by payroll taxes, invested not in production facilities but in government securities if not spent outright. The payroll tax proved insufficient to fund Medicare and now Social Security as well, so it must be supplemented by additional taxation and/or debt.

Social Security and Medicare were in the remote future for most workers. They did not provide for unemployment or extraordinary health costs before age 65. Besides, many workers might wish to supplement the income and reimbursement available through these programs. The full impact would not come until those entering the labor force at the time the legislation was enacted reached retirement age, around 1985 for Social Security, 2010 for Medicare. Much of worker saving for retirement is done late in working life. So although motivation for saving was diminished, significant decline in savings trends was not apparent in the early decades of these programs. They may have contributed to the sharp drop in savings rates in the past two decades.

Unemployment compensation, initiated by states, was enacted at the federal level in 1939. The small amount and short duration would have limited impact on savings motivation or rate.

BUSINESS PRACTICE

More recently the once strongest motivation for saving, home ownership, has been undermined by relaxation or near-elimination of down payment requirements for mortgages. Relaxation of buyer income to mortgage size limits also increased the number of home buyers whose mortgage obligations precluded saving. But it is only part of the buy now pay later (or default) mentality of the consumer revolution. Credit cards, a convenient way of handling payments, have been diverted from their basic purpose into a means of dis-saving, building up debt. The only motivation for saving that has been enhanced over the years is college education for one's children. How much college education contributes to the economy is debatable. What is not is that it defers gainful employment for years.

It is impossible to quantify the influence of each of these changes on motivation to save and on savings rates. The timing of the decline in saving is very appropriate for the change in mortgage practices and the multiplication of credit cards and card debt. It also coincides with the presumed full impact of Social Security legislation, whereas that of Medicare comes later.

SAVE OR SINK

Investment in new and better products and processes is not the only source of growth, but it will be far more important in the future than in the past. It could be the only source of growth. For the last half century, growth was largely driven by demography. With the baby boom population, nearly twice as large as its predecessor, entering the labor force, the ratio of working age population to total population kept rising. The rise in female labor force participation in the same period increased the proportion of the working age population in the labor force. Were it not for this demographic bonus, per capita incomes would not have risen.

In the future a combination of boomer retirement and increasing longevity will reverse the trend in the ratio of working to total population. Female labor force participation may not change; male has declined. We face a demographic deficit for several decades to come.

It is important to increase the savings rate. Large down payments for home mortgages are needed not just for financial health in the housing market, but as a source of saving to finance investment. For all but the biggest ticket items, such as housing, new cars, pay as you go should be the rule. Credit cards as a means of enabling owners to pile up debt - negative savings - needs restructuring. The industry, mainly banks, should set strict standards for issuing cards, and for renewing cards. Limitation of the number of cards issued to one individual would be a more difficult task. Credit cards are not to be used as money machines; there are ATMs for that.

Credit cards as a means of enabling owners to pile up debt - negative savings - needs restructuring. The industry, mainly banks, should set strict standards for issuing cards, and for renewing cards. Limitation of the number of cards issued to one individual would be a more difficult task. Credit cards are not to be used as money machines; there are ATMs for that.

Social Security and Medicare are fiscally unsound and must be reformed. In restoring Social Security financial viability it should be possible to introduce incentives to save. Retirement income need not be based exclusively on years of employment and earnings. Workers should be encouraged to supplement taxes through saving. It is not a matter of higher earnings in the market than offered by the Treasury, but of investing in economic growth. Systematic saving channeled into private investment is a much more productive way of financing health insurance than a tax model than channels taxes into government securities.

The big problem is the high and rising share of income spent on health care, not just Medicare. Here a revision of public and private insurance systems, no matter how much worth doing. Higher taxes, higher savings, is not the answer. Costs must be cut if there is to be an opportunity for saving.

The decline of saving coincided with the beginning of the high retirement-savings age of baby boomers. Present orientation is a characteristic of the culture of poverty. Savings is about the future. The alternative to a higher personal savings rate is a continuing decline in income. Incentives and penalties can go only so far. Ultimately an affluent future calls for culture change.

Chapter 8

College Education: Investment, Insurance, or Lottery?

Today many question the value of a college education. Widespread concern that college tuition is in the neighborhood of $40,000 a year is one reason there are questions whether a college education is worth the cost. Disappointment with the results: the jobs and earning of new college graduates, is another reason.

Costs of College

Most students and their parents know that a good college education need not cost more than $10,000 annual tuition, because they are paying less than that. 47% of undergraduates are attending 4-year colleges with tuition under $9,000. There is no decline in college enrollments. Furthermore, students enrolled in public universities in their states of residence are paying not much more than$10,000. The outlandish costs are for students in private universities and colleges and out of state students in public universities.

Demand and supply have adjusted to cost increases. Private universities have lost more than half their market share. Private for- profit colleges have multiplied from 10% of private college enrollment in 1990 to 36% in 2009. They lack the consumer frills, prestige, and price tag of traditional private colleges. Their growth is so rapid that private nonprofit colleges without a large endowment could end up on the endangered species list. Public 2-year community colleges over the same period increased their enrollment from 29 to 40% of the public college total. Their tuition is less than one tenth that of private colleges, about one third the in-state tuition rate for public colleges. This growing share could be an economic threat to 4-year colleges whose large freshman and sophomore classes cover losses from small upper division courses. Out of state applications to public universities have decreased and presumably so have admissions. These are the public university students who may pay astronomical tuition.

Yes, their education costs too much, but the cost is borne by the taxpayer, not the student. The cost of four years of work and income foregone is greater than the cost of going to college for most undergraduates. It is the same whatever the college of one's choice.

For-profit colleges offering courses on-line are the ultimate threat to traditional college education. Interests vested in the status quo cannot prevent the growth of this cheaper and more meritocratic way of learning. What matters eventually is what employers think. As particular programs establish a reputation by providing measures of attainment, employers will validate them, whatever lobbies and political organizations think or demand. Now that elite universities are offering online learning, the artisan practices of the past are doomed. After all, colleges replaced the tutors of old, who no doubt screamed against these new institutions that mass-taught students.

RETURNS TO EDUCATION

Is college education worth the personal investment in time and money, the taxpayer subsidy? The answer depends on the objective the student and the government have in mind. Higher education can be viewed as an aging vat, a means of reducing labor supply, production of responsible citizens, of cultured and civilized individuals, preparation for long years of unemployment and retirement. It cannot do all these things for everyone. But the drumbeat we have heard for a generation, everyone must graduate from high school, everyone must go to college, is a monotone: jobs and income. Education is the assembly line for jobs and income.

Yes, college graduates earn more than high school graduates. But they would have earned more had they not gone to college, because they are smarter. Correlation is not causation.

College graduates were 7.6% of the population 25 years of age and older in 1960, shortly before publication of Gary Becker's *Human Capital* in 1964. Now they are 30%. The value of a college degree cannot be as high today when it is commonplace than when it was the rare exception. First, the increase in supply drives down earnings and occupational choices. Second, a higher proportion of an age group going to college means a decline in average quality of college students and graduates.

With such a large increase in the educational attainment of the labor force, one would expect median earnings of full time full year workers to rise. In fact they peaked in the early 1970s and are slightly lower now.

College training for specific occupations pays off, provided the supply does not exceed the demand. Engineering, pre-med, most sciences are an investment, we know because most graduates report work in at a job that uses their college major. There is under-investment, since a high proportion of workers in these subjects are immigrants. If all college students were to major in fields with job openings, there would be an over-supply, a decline in earnings and in probability of obtaining a job in one's area of specialization. Engineering majors should thank the students who major in jobless fields.

The humanities and social sciences are more lotteries than investments since the great majority of their graduates report that their jobs are not related to their majors. But they are also an insurance policy. since the sheepskin is a device for sorting prospective hires by employers.

Assertions that the return to college education has risen in recent years are deceptive. One cannot compare the relative incomes of college and high school graduates today and decades ago, because their shares of employment have changed, and so has the distribution of occupations by educational attainment. The earnings of workers with less than a high school education have fallen. This is to be expected, since as a share of the labor force they have been declining. The proportion with only a high school diploma has also declined. Such workers have been pushed down the earnings and occupational pyramid. into lower-wage, lower-skill jobs and occupations. The share of college graduates has been rising. An increasing proportion has graduate degrees.

If the fertility rate remains below replacement in the future, then occupational and earnings prospects for college graduates could improve, as each generation will be smaller than its predecessor.

Labor Force by Educational Attainment

	Less than High School	High School,	Some College	College
1980	23.7	40.2	17.8	18.2
2010	8.9	28.8	27.7	34.6

Source: Statistical Abstract of the United States 1981 table 644; 2011, Table 593.

Employers complain of the poor preparation of students for the world of work. There are different explanations. Grade inflation, promoted by student evaluations, has tended to lower the level of effort, hence achievement. The content of a college education has become the prerogative of the student. Courses, majors have been created to accommodate student wishes. Many choose courses and majors of limited cognitive content, employment prospects, or both (I dare not name them).This is one reason why so many graduates hold jobs which bear no relation to their academic studies, jobs which do not require a college degree or college education.

There is little relation between the distribution of college graduates by major and of employment or job opening in related occupations. That is not necessarily a criticism. Preparation for the job market is not the only objective of a college education. Curricula reflect multiple objectives and interests. But then college education should not be promoted by creating false expectations. There are professional majors, programs, but they are a small share of the college curriculum and engage a small proportion of college students.

Higher education is now a zero sum game with all workers as players. Those who never go to college are the biggest losers. Many who graduate from college are better off than if they hadn't at the expense of those who did not graduate or enter. How do we know? During the period in which college graduates quadrupled as a share of the labor force, there was essentially no change in the earnings of full time full year workers. Hence, if an increasing share were better off, then an increasing share must have been made worse off.

With so many going to college, some seek to improve their chances by earning graduate degrees. Growth in graduate degrees earned has been greater than in baccalaureate degrees. In many fields there is a growing oversupply. They bump others who have only a bachelor's degree, who in turn bump others with no degree. It is not that college graduates are taking "high school" jobs, but that higher labor force educational attainment has raised the educational average of lower-skill occupations. Higher education is a positional struggle; those who have more years and degrees move to the head of the line for jobs and pay, pushing others back.

Occupational Structure

The basic implicit assumption behind the propaganda for college education is that the occupational structure will adjust to educational achievement. Double the number of college graduate and the number of professional and managerial jobs will also double. It is a fallacy of course, the fallacy of composition. What may benefit an individual does not translate into a benefit for all. Occupational structure adjusts to technology and demand, not to supply. The distribution of workers by educational attainment has changed dramatically in the last generation, as we have seen; the occupational structure has changed much less.

There is another assumption, that new technology increases the need for highly educated workers. Tell that to the Luddites. It is true up to a point, but it also destroys jobs, including jobs held by highly educated workers. The Industrial Revolution replaced skilled artisans, craftsmen with unskilled factory workers. The information/ communication revolution is doing much the same thing. Much new technology, which formerly reduced the need for manual labor, now is simplifying the work of many millions of skilled and intellectual workers.

Search engines and the Internet reduce the need for highly skilled researchers, typists no longer need know how to spell, and clerks no longer need to calculate. Bookstores are a thing of the past, and soon so will be libraries as we have known them. The print press, the publishing industry will follow in the steps of the film camera and film and its processing. Spectator activities of all sorts are under threat of extinction as their performances become available anywhere, any time.

Today's advanced technologies are being manufactured in less developed nations by poorly educated workers and their users often need less knowledge than their predecessors.

Yes, we need more college graduates in math, the sciences, engineering and medicine instead of depending on immigrants. But we are over-supplied with graduates in the humanities and the social sciences. Most of them make little use of their majors in the jobs they get, and many admit that their work does not require a college education.

It is not new technology but its contribution to the increase in discretionary incomes that permits the employment of so many doctors and lawyers, professors and entertainers, scientists and engineers. Current and future technological change may not raise productivity enough to increase the share of income available for discretionary consumption.

We do not know whether future discretionary incomes will be spent so as to increase demand for college graduates, or for graduates in this country. Most of the increase in discretionary income over the past half century was spent on health care, which grew from 5.2% of GDP in 1960 to 17.9.% in 2011. Any future gains may be concentrated on nursing homes. For the past 40 years increases in disposable income have been largely due to increases in the ratio of workers to population. As this ratio declines, disposable income may decrease, and the choice will be which expenditures to cut or eliminate.

Education and training are means for many to improve their work and economic condition. But the claim that everybody needs a high school degree, or a college degree, is based on the fallacy of composition. It is propaganda for the industry of education. An individual may be better off with more education. But the more who go to college, the poorer their job and pay prospects. It is an expensive lottery ticket. In a century of diminished expectations, egalitarianism trumps meritocracy. The surplus of college graduates will persist.

Chapter 9

MEDICAL EDUCATION AND HEALTH CARE COSTS

Health care expenditures have more than tripled as a share of GDP in the past half century, from 5.2% in 1960 to 17.9% in 2011. This gluttonous monster is scheduled to keep growing for the next 20 years as baby boomers enter the high medical cost age group. This generation is almost twice as large as its predecessor, and longer-lived. An annual health cost growth rate of 6% is predicted for the rest of the decade. Medical costs will gobble up any gains in disposable income and drive it down as the ratio of workers to population declines.

Costs must be slashed. Policies to redistribute costs between employers, employees, taxpayers are a diversion. Many things must be done. Congress can reform malpractice insurance and enhance competition in health insurance. Health care delivery must be better organized to gain efficiency, economies of scale and scope, and reduce the role of fee for service. Medicare, Medicaid and private health insurers must limit reimbursement for tests, procedures, medications on the basis of effectiveness and cost/benefit criteria.

Here I address a neglected issue on the supply side: reform of an antiquated and obsolete system of medical education that is far too costly and guarantees a growing shortage of primary care M.D.S. and high prices for specialist care.

Medical education is a monopoly whose performance has not served the public interest. Graduation rates peaked in the 1980s. They did not increase in thirty years despite population growth, aging, new medical procedures and improved insurance coverage. One fourth of practicing physicians, and rising, are graduates of foreign medical schools. The majority of residents in primary care are graduates of foreign medical schools, predominantly foreigners. We are getting other nations, often poor, to bear the costs of medical education for treating American patients. The American Association of Medical Colleges restricts supply, case proven. Its belated concession to increase medical school enrollments 17%, now perhaps 30%, will take 40 years to bear full fruit in number of practitioners. In the public interest enrollments should increase gradually with demand, not experience sudden lurches under pressure every forty years.

Overworked primary care M.D.S. are abandoning health insurance, raising prices and reducing their patient loads dramatically, or keeping insurance but requiring an annual up-front payment of $1,500 and up from each patient, also reducing their patient loads. Raising the pay of primary care M.D.S will induce many to further reduce their patient load, maintain their income while increasing leisure. It is the right policy but only for the long run. We live in the short run. Yes, much of the work of the primary care MD. can be done by physician assistants. But must they be imported too?

The current system of medical education and training is appropriate for 1900, when most physicians were general practitioners, but not for this century. In an age of specialization it trains every student to be a general practitioner, although only 2% of medical school seniors plan to follow that career. Graduates who plan to be surgeons are sentenced to five years of residence in general surgery, although few of them plan to be general surgeons, then serve additional residency in their surgical specialty. The prolonged period of education plus two to seven years of additional residency training is the main reason specialists are paid so much more than primary care M.D.S. No wonder pay and costs are excessive, shortages numerous, and so many practicing physicians are graduates of foreign medical schools. So much wasted time and knowledge.

Few specialists of any sort need nearly all the G.P. education required by medical schools or all the residency requirements. Does the ophthalmic surgeon who does cataracts really have to know about thoracic surgery, gastrointestinal surgery, surgery on arms and legs, never mind anatomy from the neck down? Does the dermatologist really have to know about pneumonia or kidney stones? What a waste of time and money for whose benefit? Not the patient's. Perhaps the purpose is to preserve practitioner status. The mantra of medicine is that the practitioner, however narrow the specialization, must know about all the human body, its structure, functioning, ailments and treatments. Many profess to believe it.

Similar instances of cultural stagnation have been dissected by Thomas Kuhn in his *The Structure of Scientific Revolutions*. Alternatively, this monopoly has been abused with disregard for the public interest. Medical school faculty is one beneficiary. It is a rent-demanding monopoly.

It is the generalist: the GP, internal medicine specialist, family physician who needs most medical education and in particular who requires the most time and effort to keep up with changing knowledge. It is the generalist who should have the longest period of education. All medical students who opt for a specialty early in their medical school enrollment could have an abbreviated curriculum, greatly abbreviated for some narrow specialties. Alternatively, why should 125 medical schools and rising all educate for general practice? Some medical schools might train specialists in particular fields. All those opting for a surgical specialty need spend less time as residents in general surgery, some hardly any time at all. Years would be saved, graduates would not be so heavily indebted. Entering medical school in the junior year of college, as done in most countries, would also save on education costs and time.

If generalists spend as much time in training/residency as specialists, they may earn as much as specialists. That would help terminate the shortage of primary care M.D.S. and reduce our need for immigrant physicians. If primacy care M.D.S were not 25% of the total, but closer to the European 50%, and if specialists were not practicing primary care, the quality of care would improve and costs would decline.

What is an M.D. whose interest and most of whose practice is in a particular specialty doing as a primary care MD? Given current shortages of primary care physicians, it is a common practice. He/she is likely to have forgotten much, failed to keep up. Besides, the specialization may amount to a conflict of interest, and the cognitive approach, problem-solving, may not be appropriate for the diagnostic duties of a primary care M.D. The specialist should be licensed to practice his/her specialty. not free to practice general medicine, as is now the case.

New health care legislation substantially increases the demand for medical care. It can only increase shortages, reduce access, raise prices; so does the aging of the baby boomers.

There will be a large increase in medical school enrollments. But the number of college seniors applying to medical school peaked in the 1990s, and the percentage has dropped below 2%. It must be increased to 3% if not higher to avoid decline in quality of medical students and graduates. Not as many top students are applying to medical school as they once did.

Quality of admissions declined following the last big increase of medical school enrollments in the 1970s. First, the quality of college graduates declined as there was a large increase in the proportion of the age group completing college. Second, the applicant pool shrank as a proportion of college seniors. Third, a school system in which 95% of first-time student test takers pass is not compatible with adequate quality control. Fourth, the attrition rate, which was in the 13-15% range before the last large increase in medical school enrollment in the 1970s, dropped to only 4%. This minimal attrition, plus the legendary long work day and week of residents, may contribute to the incidence of malpractice that helps drive up costs.

Cutting the years of medical education and training means much lower cost, and more years of practice. It would induce many more good students to apply for medical school and allow growth in enrollment without decline in quality. There is no other way other than importing most of our M.D.S. The casual suggestion that the government pay for medical education is not a response, it is an evasion that would add the costs of medical school to the juggernaut of health care costs.

Some large state, if not the national organization, could set up its own system of medical education, residency, licensing and certification. It would introduce curriculum and training choices appropriate for this century, radically cutting the cost in time and money for the education of most specialists, and eliminating the gap in pay between primary care M.D.S. and specialists. There would be improved access and large savings in medical costs. In time other states, medical schools and M.D.S. would have to react. The UK is going further: de-medicalizing narrow specialties, greatly reducing time and cost of training. In the U.S, this could be accomplished step by step, whether by a large state. HMOs, or Medicare and Medicaid, circumventing the monopoly stranglehold of the medical industry. It would require reform of malpractice legislation, now proceeding state by state.

Reform takes time to make a difference. There are other ways of cost control in the meantime. Much diagnosis, prescription, evaluation follow-up can be done by computer with overseas M.D.S. Procedures costing above a certain amount in the United States could be performed in approved facilities elsewhere. Private insurance, and ideally also Medicare and Medicaid, would pay for the procedure, including necessary travel costs, and save money in the process. The nations chosen would be better off. Instead of losing their M.D.S. to the United States, they would retain them and their income and receive some of their medical services. Furthermore, such a practice would stimulate investment in their medical facilities and education.

Without an adequate supply of M.D.S, primary care physicians in particular, ready access and high quality medical care are unavailable for many people, and prices are bound to rise. Without a large reduction in the cost of medical care, levels of living will continue to decline. Reform of medical education to cut the cost and increase the supply is part of the answer. It is also recognition of the reality of medical practice. The training of specialists is already a double-decker. The findings of the current explosion of biological research cannot be added as a triple-decker. Grey-haired residents?

Chapter 10

CONSUMERISM

In a few generations advanced societies have progressed from arduous labor to provide for the urgent needs of the people to focus on demand for new goods and services not previously available. Today wants and needs must be created in order to produce and market an endless stream of gimmicks and gizmos the need for which had not been previously felt by consumers.

The inventor, innovator, once the creator of valuable new products and services, is now often the creator of wants and needs which allow the productive machinery of society to continue churning out goods and jobs. What started as work ethic has been transformed to ego massage and hedonic addiction, a tyranny of consumption. Producer-oriented society has become the empire of the consumer.

Americans work longer hours per year than any other country except South Korea. Our retirement age for pension purposes is among the highest in the world, it is rising, and for most, there is no compulsory retirement age at all. The standard working day, week, year has not changed since 1938, despite a large increase in income per worker, while the proportion of the working age population in the labor force has increased substantially. It is not because we are slow, inefficient, or because we are poor and trying to catch up. On the contrary, our income is so high because we have been overworking. Why? Long ago what were once considered the necessities of life came within the reach of nearly all, and the share of income spent on them has declined to a minor part of the typical budget. But we are compulsive consumers with a taste for novelty.

IDENTITY

Until recently, for most people, identity was associated with job and occupation. In the past these changed little during a lifetime, often were inherited. The practice can be indicated by the distribution of family names in the past. English names were (and are) predominantly occupation names: Smith, Farmer, Fisher, Miller, Baker, Carpenter, and other occupational names account for the majority of the population of English ancestry.

Today, with a much more educated labor force, increased mobility, and changing occupational demand associated with rapid technological and fashion change, job and occupation now lack the lifelong stability and attachment they once had. But it is not this aspect of the economy that has converted production-oriented identity to consumption orientation, but the large increase in incomes which allows most people some or a great deal of discretionary consumption, allowing them to differentiate themselves as well as to conform via their choices of consumption.

The member of the consumer culture derives his identity from the clothes he wears, the car he drives, the house he lives in and the assorted objects he displays in it. Less easily displayed is the college one attended, the group memberships, the people one knows. These change as his income rises, as fashions come and go, as his taste develops, thus so does the individual they define. We are commodity-people, compulsive consumers subject to an entertainment imperative. But consumerism is not a religion, just a contagious obsession.

CONSUMERISM

Consumerism is as old as civilization. But until recently it was confined to royal courts, a tiny elite, an incipient merchant class. Most people were preoccupied with subsistence, not possession and display. Male-dominated societies have always regarded some women as commodities, providing sex, progeny, and household labor. So women have long decorated themselves - packaged as more enticing goods. Some periods, some cultures, have been described as male-vanity cultures - men too are so preoccupied with appearance, self-presentation - that they view themselves as commodities in the eyes of others. But even then, most men could not afford the luxury to participate.

Now the consumer culture has been democratized. It has crowded out producer culture in most minds. Most people can afford the time and resources to participate at various levels of their own choosing, and most do. Look at teenagers, twenty-something today - they have formed a male vanity culture en masse. Most consumers also produce, but only as a requirement for consumption. The unsatiated or possibly unsatiable demand for more consumption drives many toward enterprise, risk-taking and work.

J. M. Keynes reasoned that with rising real incomes, an increased proportion of income would be saved, a declining proportion spent on consumption. American households saved 8-10% of their income decades ago, only 2-3% in the past decade with substantially higher incomes. and peak labor force participation. Yes, easy home loans, Social Security and Medicare have reduced the need for saving, but there was little will. All that work, all that income, was not sufficient to sate the hunger for consumer goods and services.

Investors, innovators need demand for their products to survive. But they also need capital to invest in new products and services. Scant household savings have been supplemented by flows of capital from other nations.

The basic core of economics is what Boulding called the Pig Principle: more is better. But its applicability is extremely limited, to fungible goods, specifically money. For though 2 TV sets are better than one, it is not at all clear that 10 are better than 5. There are limits to human ability to consume any particular good or service.

There are ingenious ways of circumventing saturation of consumer desires: many invest not in consumer items, but in collections, whether baseball cards or Picassos or stamps or whatever can grow almost indefinitely. We are evolving from an economy of consumers to a society of collectors. Consumption once meant using up, or at least using; collectors do neither; they simply hoard, absent any precautionary motive, merely as a tangible extension of themselves. The rare individuals who do not seem able to stop accumulating items of the same kind, the famous 3,000 pairs of shoes of Imelda Marcos, are pathological cases.

The motivation to consume is diverse. At one extreme is Veblen's conspicuous consumption, a means of displaying your superiority to others. Boulding might call it the Peacock Principle. The desire to be different, to stand out, supports demand for novelty. At the other extreme is narcissistic consumption, purely self-satisfying without regard to others. In between is imitative consumption, keeping up with the Joneses, the wish to conform. In our society, novelty becomes the norm to which one should conform. Many consumers are driven by both motives at the same time: novelty-seeking as conformity, a self-perpetuating cycle of display. These are social motivations.

There are those who need prestigious or distinctive products or labels as psychological armor to protect self-esteem. But there is also the simple pleasure of possession, accumulation, an objectified response to uncertainly, a sense of insecurity, but often a tribute to a sense of the aesthetic. These may be purely personal, or also for display. And then there is plain consumption serving the needs of subsistence and safety. Conspicuous consumption promotes novelty and hence invention, but discourages innovation, the spread of novelty. Imitative or positional consumption promotes innovation, and speeds up the rate of adoption of new inventions. Narcissistic consumption has no impact on innovation or invention. Given demand for novelty, new wants are readily created and propagated.

LIMITED GOODS

There are space-intensive goods, and there are time-intensive goods. How many closets, china cabinets, and chests of drawers do you fill? More comes at increased cost: a larger house. or a second home. As to time goods, there is no way of expanding waking hours or assuring longer life or longer vacations. Travel and education are very time-intensive goods. How much time can one spend on cruises, how often can one dine out?

There are limits to the supply of specific goods and services; as well as limits to demand. Most goods and services are indefinitely reproducible. But some are physically limited, some are socially limited. The supply of some kinds of goods cannot be expanded at all, or only at the sacrifice of quality. There are only so many violins made in Cremona centuries ago. Some now sell for millions of dollars. Rising incomes increase their prices, not their supply. They can be played, but there are many other items collectors prize that only serve the purpose of owner pride or display. And there are quality differences in many services, real or by reputation. Whether these are the best heart surgeons or best lawyers or string quartet or baseball players or plumbers, again higher incomes simply drive up prices, increase inequality. The best is not reproducible.

The demand for designer labels, whether in clothing or in college education, the passion to collect antiques, fine art, conspicuous consumption, cannot be fully satisfied. Insofar as demand is for exclusion, increased supply devalues the service or product. An increase in the supply of beachfront cottages soon causes crowding and pollution. The prestigious vacation, the process of suburbanization, drives up the prices and reduces quality of all these physically or socially limited goods and services, and increases the share of income devoted to their acquisition. It also imposes costs on others: higher prices, lower quality, or the onus of exclusion: a sort of Hindu caste system in a materialist world. Income available for consumption of other goods and services ceases to grow, and may decline.

THE FUTURE OF CONSUMERISM?

We are nearing the time when despite the imagination of inventors and innovators an increasing share of effort and expenditure is being devoted to acquisition of goods and services that are not indefinitely reproducible, to socially or physically limited goods. In this sort of world interest in progress may decline, and with it the willingness to finance research.

The decline in fertility and rising life expectancy poses a different kind of threat to the future of progress. Lower fertility reflects the conflict between rearing of children and the compulsion to consume. Children are no longer producer goods, as they were on the farm. With pensions and Social Security and Medicare, they are no longer the essential reliance of the aged.

How does increased longevity affect the future of progress? It is the young, not the old, who are novelty-seeking. Redistribution of income from the working age population to the aged retired will diminish demand for the new and different. diverting resources that might otherwise be devoted to investment and research. Production orientation will obviously decline. Will the values, motivations, institutions that undergird scientific and technical progress be diluted to ineffectiveness?

Low fertility has other consequences: an oversupply of durable goods. Many households have no children, no heirs to whom to leave their homes, furniture, and other durable goods. With greater longevity, even those who have heirs find that their heirs are middle-aged, well supplied with durables. Second hand markets will grow, new ones will be created. The need for new durables will decline, reducing employment in their production, reducing income as well. The lower cost of second hand durables releases some household income for other uses. But this prospect depends on the willingness of future generations to satisfy their needs and desires for durable goods from existing stocks rather than new production.

How much affluence do we need, and for what?

Chapter 11

DEPRESSION IN THE HOUSEHOLD ECONOMY

Income per capita may have been declining in the United States for a generation, but the statisticians don't know it. What has happened is a dramatic shrinkage in the household economy, which is not included in the GDP or measures of personal income. Production of goods and services in the household for its own consumption has been shifted in large part to the marketplace, where it is counted.

How can we compare household output of goods and services for its own use in the past with today? It may be an impossible task. But there are several indicators that give a rough idea of the change. One is the change in size and composition of households. The other is the increase in labor force participation of women. A working woman has less time for housework, and more money to buy the goods and services she might have produced for herself and her family.

Household size matters. It averaged 3.4 during the post-WWII period until 1964, declined to 2.5, is now some 2.7, a response to the prolonged recession. Household composition matters. Non-family households have increased from ten percent of the total in 1940 to 35% today. Married couples with children, 44.5% of households in 1960, are now only 20.2%. Single person households have increased in the same period from 13 to 27% of households.

If a household has 4 or more members, it makes sense to cook 2 or 3 means a day from cheap basic ingredients. There are economies of scale. But if the household has only one or two members, it makes more sense to eat out or buy prepared foods often, unless it is too poor to do so. A household with two or more adults is much more likely to be able to care for sick members at home than one with a single adult, who may have to relegate them to hospitals, nursing homes.

Thus what remains of the household economy lacks the economies or scale it once had. Residences themselves have become less efficient as they have shrunk in numbers of occupants but increased in floor space. A household of 2 persons cannot be as efficiently operated as one with 4. Costs of heating and cooling in particular are much higher on a per capita basis. Fortunately computers and electronic toys came along just in time to keep single children occupied and single parents entertained. For every solution there is a problem.

Smaller(and single-adult) households lack the capacity to provide some goods and services which large households can render; and they are less efficient in those they can provide. In the past many patients were taken care of at home, now they go to hospitals and nursing homes. They contribute significantly to the increased costs of medical care. The same is true of the increasing number of elderly people who are disabled. Today they are much more likely than in the past to be institutionalized. Smaller households are not the only factor; health insurance has reduced the need and incentive.

Take food. In the past most meals were eaten at home, prepared from basic ingredients. Only the cost of the ingredients was included in the GDP. Now many more meals are eaten out, and more home meals are purchased already prepared. Why cook for one or two if It takes as much time and effort as for three or four, but there are fewer cooks and helpers?

Take child care. Today many children go to day camps, nearly all are in kindergarten. In the past there were no day camps, and most children stayed at home until first grade. Most never completed high school, now most start college. Laws in most states requiring school attendance to high school graduation or age 18 have increased the burdens of child rearing, one factor in the decline in fertility. Children in school have less time to work at home.

Much other work around the household which once was performed by its members has been shifted to the market and the notice of statisticians: yard work, clothes washing and ironing, painting. Another partial measure of the size of the household economy and the magnitude of the shift toward the market economy, is the proportion of women of working age not in the labor force, and the decline in that percentage in recent decades. It was 33.9% in 1950, rising to a peak of 60% in 1999. This increase contributed to growth in the market economy and per capita market income. It was amplified by the increase in college education of women, who now outnumber men in graduating classes, upgrading their occupational distribution and earnings. But it was a one-time boost that is over.

The issue of causality is beyond our scope. There has been a substantial loss of economies of scale in the household sector, increased education and greater occupational opportunities for women. Perhaps the WWII experience of “Rosie the Riveter” and others who replaced men in uniform was a factor.

Despite all the promotion of economic growth, we really have been on a treadmill for the past forty years. We have to keep on pedaling just to stay in place, and may have to pedal faster as the cost of resources rises.

The growing share of the population 65 and over and retired has the potential of reversing some of the decline in the household economy. They have time on their hands, often are looking for something to do, and in most cases could use the extra income obtainable indirectly by supplying some of the goods and services they have been accustomed to buy. They would be self-employed but not subject to the minimum wage or the payroll tax. Nor would the non-cash income they may generate be hostage to the Internal Revenue Service.

Time series of income overstate growth because they refer only to the market economy. International comparisons of income also refer to the market economy. Inclusion of the household would reduce the difference between rich and poor countries. A country with low per capita market income that is not over-populated may have a household economy that provides most of its needs for food, fuel, shelter, transportation. Its principal shortcomings are education and health care. National growth rates accompanied by urbanization shift labor and resources from the household to the market economy, overstating the growth in income.

Chapter 12

OBSOLESCENCE AND EMPLOYMENT: ARE MORE JOBS NECESSARY?

High labor force participation, a long working life, will help pay for the pensions and health care of the aged. But will the jobs be performed by humans or by robots that (or who) receive no wages and pay no taxes? If the ratio of capital to labor increases too much it may be necessary to shift the tax burden from earnings to capital assets.

Do we really need so much labor? Consider the household dependency ratio – the number of dependents divided by the number of workers. During the baby boom generation, there were roughly three children per household (actually per female of child-bearing age). Now there are not quite two. Furthermore, with fewer children, a higher proportion of women are in the labor force than in the past. For many a smaller house today with lower operating costs would be just as adequate. But new houses are larger than the old. There are new gadgets to buy, but their cost is tiny compared to the cost of rearing and educating children. The need for income should be lower than in the past to maintain the same standard of living. Households should have higher savings rates but they have much lower rates.

We over-consume. The commodities we buy range in life expectancy from the highly perishable, foods that must be consumed in days if not refrigerated, to houses that can last for centuries. As our incomes have risen, we have accumulated the more durable goods. Quite a few people own a second home. Most own only one house, but it is much bigger than in the past. Many households own more than one car. There are practical limits to the accumulation of multiple units of bulky durables - they add to clutter, fulfill no useful function. Who needs, who wants multiple stoves, refrigerators, washers? Furniture: chairs, tables, beds, chests etc. are more collectible than stoves and dishwashers, but their bulk constrains their number. Few households own more than one car per driver. Paintings, carpets, which are 2-dimensional, are more conveniently collected in substantial numbers and their accumulation adds to aesthetic and decorative value. Clothing, jewelry also lend themselves to large collections. At the other extreme, stocks and bonds occupy no space and are indefinitely additive.

The strategy of accumulation of material things without converting one's home into a warehouse is turnover. It is both a household consumer tactic and a business producer strategy. High turnover means high demand for new products, high employment in their production. Low turnover, as we experienced during the great depression, followed by WWII which devoted industrial production to war needs, means low production and employment.

How long does the average car last? Few know, because they sell it for a newer car long before it dies. Houses outlive any occupant. But old houses had no central heating or air conditioning, just several fireplaces and a porch. They had no garage. Some had lead pipes connected to the water supply. Roofs have to be replaced eventually, electric systems upgraded. Yet we see many old houses, fully upgraded, perfectly livable by current standards, torn down and replaced by bigger and presumably better houses.

How long should we hold on to all but the highly perishable before replacing them? Most commodities have maintenance costs. Car parts break down and must be repaired or replaced. When these costs rise above some level it is time to buy another car. We used to darn socks, but not today. Socks are very cheap, and darning is a lot of trouble. We still resole some shoes. At some stage in their depreciation we do not go for another re-soling and re-heeling, but throw them away. It is fair to say that we tend to replace many durable commodities too soon, before maintenance costs become a factor. For some durables it is not maintenance costs but quality of performance that limits their useful life. Fabrics fade, become threadbare, tire treads wear away. For others, it is style. Men formerly wore felt hats; women's skirt lengths kept changing.

Human longevity and low fertility have tended to increase turnover. There is the multi-generational cycle: newly married, children, empty nest. But the nest is not empty of the beds formerly occupied, or the chests of drawers. By the time the parents move to smaller quarters, or leave this world, the children have acquired furniture and housing of their own. They have little room for inherited bulky durable goods. When families averaged 4 or 5 children there was less problem, more heirs per household. When parents died younger, their children's needs were greater, they had yet to accumulate a houseful of durable goods. The supply of inheritable goods is increasing, but children's demand for them has fallen.

Turnover is accomplished in two ways: selling or discarding. Inheritance could be regarded as delayed turnover.

There are markets for discarded goods. The real estate market for used homes, used car markets, are well organized. Few houses or cars are trashed by their owners when they no longer want them. But second hand markets for used TVs, dishwashers, lawnmowers are very limited or altogether absent. The value of such used items is too low, they are bulky, there is little profit to be made. For most durables there are flea markets. Charitable organizations, Salvation Army, distribute goods to needy people, or can afford to sell goods which were acquired free of charge. The donor is reimbursed by the IRS through itemized charitable deductions from income tax; call it a Federal government flea market. The deduction is likely to be eliminated, but the organizations and the process will continue, on a reduced scale perhaps.

What would happen if first buyers retained their cars (or TVs or refrigerators) twice as long? The used price would go down substantially, and some former used car buyers might become new car buyers. But the demand for new cars would decline. If there were no used car market, then demand for new cars would fall by half. There must be a billion beds in this country just in households, plus more in hotels. Do we need to produce any beds for the next 50 years?

Why produce a new model every year? If new models were three years apart, there would be savings in costs of production, in advertising costs, and very likely slower turnover by customers who are model or style-conscious. Would there be any reduction in technological change? Probably not, but research and development might be more efficient. There would be no need for marginal improvements this year, only sometime in the next three years.

How to maintain production and employment? Buyers must be induced to discard their durable goods promptly, the sooner the better. This can be done in two ways: making new models superior to and perhaps cheaper than the old, or by changes in appearance that render the old product obsolete. When depreciated goods are discarded by their original owner, are they just trashed, or are they traded to others at discount prices? Trashing means demand for replacement production and jobs; trading down does not. They require different levels of employment, different levels of consumer income.

Obsolescence is created by technical change. Old houses had no electricity, no air conditioning, no garages. These could be added in some cases, or the house itself could be replaced. Old cars had no seat belts, or air bags, windows had to be rolled up and down by hand, the doors locked and unlocked likewise.

But obsolescence can also be created by style change and psychological manipulation of owners and customers. Consumer satisfaction with computers, portable phones, seasonal clothing styles can be undermined without any reduction in their performance. A woman's skirt is too long or short, a man's tie too narrow or wide, the entire wardrobe is yesterday's style and should be replaced by today's, although it has barely been worn. What is the color of the season or year?

If consumers find that they are spending less on acquisition of durables as a result of longer product life, would there be a significant decline in demand for labor, higher unemployment or adjustment in hours of work, retirement age? We do not know. Some of the money saved would be spent for goods and services that consumers could not afford in the past. But some of the saving would be converted into commodity-free leisure.

More leisure would be in line with historical trends since the industrial revolution. Labor work time declined from 12 hours a day 6 days a week, essentially no vacation or retirement, to the 8-hour day, 40-hour week in 1938, together with social security. This trend was reversed by the large increase in the labor force participation of women from 1960 to 1990, but this increase was largely a shift of labor from the household economy to the market. Meanwhile post-retirement leisure grew rapidly with longevity. Increase in educational attainment has raised the average age of labor force entry, substituting education, not leisure, for labor.

Do we really need so much labor? Consider the household dependency ratio – the number of dependents divided by the number of workers. During the baby boom generation, there were roughly three children per household (actually per female of child-bearing age). Now there are not quite two. Furthermore, with fewer children, a higher proportion of women are in the labor force than in the past. For many a smaller house with lower operating costs would be just as adequate. But new houses are larger than the old. There are new gadgets to buy, but their cost is tiny compared to the cost of rearing and educating children. The need for income should be lower than in the past to maintain the same standard of living. Households should have higher savings rates but they have much lower rates.

As long as consumer demand for novelty and distinction prevails, or can be created, producers will deliver. They have limited incentive to design goods to last. A change in attitudes, a change in behavior, would reduce our need for income and labor, increase our leisure. It would lessen the burden of an aging population on its workers.

Chapter 13

INEQUALITY

Political life in a democracy is an eternal struggle between conflicting concepts of equality - meritocracy and egalitarianism, equality of achievement vs. equality of opportunity. The private economy is meritocratic, as judged by the consumer. It requires competition and information. Egalitarianism in the marketplace spells failure. The economy generates income. The government is egalitarian, it redistributes income and provides services by taxing and spending.

Inequality of wealth is a small part of the answer. Since high earners save much more than the poor, they account for most inherited wealth. Thus inequality breeds inequality. In the past, when the average family had 3 or more children, inherited wealth tended to dissipate; now that it has barely two, there could be little dissipation other than through estate taxation. But public concern is with worker incomes and their inequality. They are earned, wealth may not be. Why are there large differences in inequality among advanced nations? Why has inequality changed over time in the United States? Each country, each time period, is sui generis. But the division of employment between the public and the private sectors is a major factor. Pay structure in the market sector tends toward the meritocratic; in the public sector it tends toward the egalitarian. The larger the public sector, the more equal is income distribution. Thus many European countries have low inequality, as did the United States during WWII.

A second factor is the extent of unionization of the labor force in the private sector, but also in the public sector. It tends toward egalitarianism. Firms and industries that are unionized will have a pat structure closer to the public sector than those that are not. Unions raise the floor of pay and reduce the range. This is also likely to be true of deferred compensation (pensions) and contingent compensation, such as health insurance benefits. Teachers unions in the public sector have the same effect but limited to an occupation.

In the United States, employment in the public sector has changed very little as a share of total employment except in periods of war, even though public spending has varied substantially. The United States had an egalitarian distribution of income in WWII because so much of the labor force was on public payrolls. As to unionization, it has grown in the public sector, dropped dramatically in the private sector, with a net effect of increasing inequality. Both shares are much higher in Europe than here, perhaps the main explanation for differences in inequality.

Third, one should examine occupational distribution and changes in this distribution, since different occupational groups have quite different distributions. Laborers and other low skill workers will have low inequality; if their share of the labor force declines, inequality will rise. Have declines in the number in unskilled and low skill occupations, and/or increase in numbers in occupations with more unequal pay distribution accounted for a significant increase in inequality? It is a complex question.

Extreme inequality is found in occupations such as professional sports and entertainment, including music, painting, and the like. These are occupations which many regard as hobbies. Those working for a living compete with capable amateurs who are prepared to work for nothing. Earnings in these occupations are also characterized by a high level of uncertainty. In most cases, output is attributable to individuals, not a group product. What distinguishes them from most occupations is the fact that a worker's output or product is scalable: it can be multiplied, or it can be amplified. Amplification means that good performers can reach large audience via modern communication technology and name recognition. In many cases it is their output that is scalable: records of musical performances, replicas of visual arts can be multiplied. Since consumer span of attention is limited; there is very little room at the top. Attention is focused on very few players, performers. For everyone who makes it to the top there will be several just as good, but no room.

Occupations whose workers are paid by the hour are more equal in distribution than occupations whose workers are paid by the product or job. The latter are occupations in which performance is that of individual workers rather than products of companies, large organizations. In many cases the product is scalable. In spectator sports it is the amplification of audience via TV, and advertising revenue, that results in million dollar salaries for top players. The market for recordings of past games is very small. On the other hand in the visual arts, multiplication is dominant. In music, both effects are important: audience amplification via radio and TV, and reproduction on tape, discs.

This cause of inequality started with Gutenberg for multiplication, Marconi for amplification. But it is advances in information and communication technology in the past half century that have contributed most to inequality. After WWII, the visual dimension of TV free to viewers, but not to advertisers, was added to the auditory dimension of radio. Now reproduction technology can record sound and sight of any form of entertainment, creating multiple originals by the same artist. Neither time nor distance is a barrier. Neither serves as protective tariff for local enterprise. It may contribute more to inequality in the United States than in Europe because its national market is much larger.

Information both better and more accessible generates a reputation effect in some services, doctors and lawyers for example. Such services are typically very expensive and their value can have either a positive or a negative sign. Individual reputation earns a premium. Their product is not scalable but their reputation can raise their value as well as demand for their services. Thus even in some non-scalable occupations, the information and communication revolution has probably increased income inequality.

How much has multiplication, amplification, reputation increased income inequality in particular occupations, and how much has this increase raised overall inequality? We do not know. To reiterate, the inequality considered is labor earnings inequality. It does not refer to incomes of those not working. Nor does it reflect the actions of government to redistribute income via taxation and expenditure policies.

Division of employment between the market and the public sectors, unionization, occupational distribution and occupational characteristics may account for changes in distribution or for international differences in distribution. But they cannot fully account for the prevailing distribution. Other factors must be considered. Education in particular can reduce inequality. With an under-educated labor force the pay for highly skilled and professional workers must be a large multiple of that of the unskilled, in both business and government, if they are to employ and retain the workers needed for the job. As education and training improve, inequality can decline. Large scale immigration of low skill workers in recent decades has increased inequality. The industry structure, always changing, will have some effect. Some are human capital-intensive., others are not. Accounting for inequality in any case is not justification.

Culture influences the primary distributions mentioned above, but its principal role is in redistribution. Socialist parties have never gained traction in the United States, whereas all European nations have major socialist parties, which have gained power at some time in most nations. American culture is biased toward meritocracy; European culture toward egalitarianism. Perhaps it is because Europe was a feudal society of class and privilege not so long ago, whereas America for most of its history has been a frontier society.

Circumstances matter. When incomes are growing and opportunity is abundant, inequality is accepted. But with static or declining incomes and restricted opportunities, inequality becomes the paramount issue of social discord.

Chapter 14

EGALITARIANISM OR LIFE AS A LOTTERY

America's egalitarian crusaders are terminally corrupt. They send their children to private schools and elite universities, the refuge of the meritocratic elite. This alternative must be eliminated.

Not all schools or colleges are equal. Not all jobs and occupations are equal. There is no equal pay. Not all brides or grooms are equal. Life is unfair. If inequality is inevitable, at least its distribution can be fair. There is one way, only one way, to distribute fairly the limited supplies of the best things in life. That is by lottery.

Students should be assigned to schools in a district by lottery; thus one school is little better than another. This is already done in South Korea. But South Korea is egalitarian only in opportunity; it is cruelly meritocratic in achievement.

All students must be promoted on schedule, as most are already. All should graduate from high school. Test-taking is minimized, eliminated where possible, for the sake of equal treatment of teachers as well as of students. On graduation almost everyone is a valedictorian, with 30 seconds for a valedictory. Some school districts, some states are still holding out, but most have fallen into line.

Spelling bees and other competitions have winners and losers. It is not possible to select winners by chance, so these competitions have been abolished in some states, eventually in all. Somehow sports have escaped the clutch of egalitarianism, but in time they will have to be eliminated since there are winners, and losers who may suffer some decline in self-esteem. Competitive sports should be limited to professional athletes, whose performance can remind us of the evil ways of our ancestors, the cowboys and evildoers, the tyrants and their victims, all strivers for narcissistic superiority.

For others, there must be affirmative action for short people in basketball, for small people in football, for stupid people in chess.

The Woodrow Wilson High School of Science and Technology in northern Virginia, one of the nation's best, is about to be euthanized. It is very selective, and egalitarians complain that some ethnic groups are under-represented. By the same token, other ethnic groups are over-represented. Selectivity is a sin.

It so happens that among residents in its affluent service area, some ethnic groups are over-represented, others under-represented. This itself is unfair. So we must apply national ethnic proportions to determine fairness in ethnic representation. Alternatively the school should be relocated to a service area with a different ethnic mix.

Everyone goes to college, assigned by lottery. On graduation, the job lottery is complicated. One cannot assign art majors to engineering jobs. There must be lotteries major by major. A surplus in any major is assigned to the lottery pool for jobs that require no college education. A shortage is filled by immigrants.

Anyone can be president is our credo, but not everyone can be. But thousands can share that honor now that presidential terms are limited to one day. Presidential elections have been replaced by the presidential lottery. There is a problem, a shortage of candidates who are willing make the trip to the White House for a single night, sign a few papers, perhaps make a speech, then return home to preside over the inauguration of their presidential bookshelf.

What egalitarians do not understand is the law of supply. If there are millions of valedictorians, thousands of ex-presidents, their titles have no value, they do not represent an achievement. The ideal egalitarian society is one of zero achievement, zero value.

Education and politics are now truly egalitarian. The marriage market must be replaced by a marital lottery. Who should wed the most attractive brides, the most desirable grooms? We reject the dowry system of India or the bride-price practice of Africa. Instead, would-be brides and grooms pick a number from the appropriate wedding bowl. There are different bowls for different age groups but no other way of gaming the system. Seniors may not pick from the youngsters' bowl. Sorry Muslims, one number only. Multiculturalism is for the classroom.

Justice is blind.

Chapter 15

LIVING ON $3,650 A YEAR IN THE USA

The federal income tax personal exemption for a single individual is $3,650. For two individuals filing jointly, it is $7,300. The full time worker averages around 2,000 hours per year. Thus the personal exemption is equivalent to a wage of $1.825 per hour for a single individual, between $1.825 and $3.65 for two filing jointly, depending on whether they hold one or two full time-equivalent jobs. The federal minimum wage is $7.25 an hour. Federal tax laws conflict with federal wage laws. Reconciliation is proposed that would simplify income taxes and the lives of taxpayers.

Who could survive on $3,650 per year? Someone living on the land, paying no property taxes, raising his own food and fuel, drawing water from a well in front, using an outhouse in the back yard, with a horse, grass-fed, to pull his plow and fertilize the field, no electricity, no tickets to football games or symphony orchestras.

Yes, there is a glimmer of recognition of the absurdity of the personal exemption: the standard deduction, larger than the personal exemption, is $5,800 for a single individual, $11,600 for a couple filing jointly. The sum of personal exemption and standard deduction yields an annual income of $9,450 for one and of $18,900 for two filing jointly. These sums are still equivalent to an hourly wage of $4.725 for a single worker if both work full time, up to $$9.450 if only one works, for couples filing jointly

MINIMUM WAGE

The same congress enacts legislation establishing a federal minimum wage, currently $7.25 an hour, equivalent to an annual income of $14.500 for a single individual, $29,000 for two individuals. It is raised periodically to reflect increases in cost of living. Federal tax laws conflict with wage laws..

At one time proponents of a higher minimum argued for a wage sufficient to support a family of four, which was never enacted. Those days are long gone, now that most women are in the work force, a high proportion of households are single-person, and fertility rates have fallen. Let us suppose that minimum wages are now intended to support the worker. Perhaps many workers could scrape by on $14,000 a year provided they live in small towns or the countryside. Why the inconsistency between minimum wage and federal income tax personal exemption? Why perpetuation of such an unrealistic exemption? Why maintain a standard deduction as a devious way of partial correction for failure of personal exemptions to reflect costs of living?

The personal exemption should be linked to the minimum wage, but not necessarily equal to it. If equal, two persons filing jointly would pay no tax on the first $29.000 of income. The minimum wage is a comparison point, not a benchmark. The personal exemption allows for dependents, which the minimum wage does not. The minimum wage reflects productivity, which personal exemption does not. But much the same considerations should be involved.

ITEMIZED DEDUCTIONS

The standard deduction would be eliminated or incorporated in the personal exemption. Schedule A, itemized deductions, should be scrapped. There are commitments that should not have been made but should be honored, but no new commitments made. All subsidies should be eliminated, especially charitable donations, home mortgage interest. What to do about medical costs depends on the future of health insurance.

What was once the main source of federal tax revenue has become an instrument of social values, virtue, redistribution, also known as theft. Itemized deductions cost revenue. So do other tax exemptions and cuts embedded in the tax code. That is one reason for unrealistic personal exemptions; revenue must be made up. Workers too poor to buy a house or a new electric car or donate to charity pay higher taxes to counter the revenue lost to subsidies. So do renters, public transit riders and skinflints. The subsidy on home mortgage interest depends on one's income tax bracket - the higher the bracket, the larger the tax saving. It is regressive.

There are many more tax breaks scattered around various tax forms, most of which should go, including the 15% capital gains tax rate that benefits billionaires. One outcome would be lower tax rates combined with high tax revenue. Some of these subsidies, for activities and products that cannot survive without subsidy, are truly harmful to the economy as well as to taxpayers not collecting them. There is a place for subsidies, on their own merits, but they should stand alone and bear scrutiny, not sneak into the federal income tax.

Any items on Schedule A retained, such as casualty, theft, possibly medical, belong in Schedule 1040. Please, no more worksheets; perhaps a statutory limit on the number of worksheets.

Without a standard deduction, and much reduced itemized deductions, there would be considerable savings in record keeping, calculation, time, cost and error on the part of taxpayers, but also on the part of the IRS. There would be less work for tax lawyers. The IRS estimates that taxpayers spend over three million uncompensated unhappy man-years preparing their federal income tax returns. That is between 2 and 3 percent of total employment man-hours. It is a wasted resource. Households also pay HR Block and other tax preparers to finish their job. The cost of paying taxes is exorbitant and should be slashed. Eliminating itemized deductions would be a big help.

With personal exemptions reflecting the minimum wage, the minimum taxable income would rise. The progressivity of the current tax structure would be increased slightly. The larger the personal exemption, the steeper the curve of progressivity of a given rate. Fewer brackets might be used to achieve the same revenue resulting from today's 6 brackets.

There is nothing sacred about current progressivity, it could be higher or lower. The federal income tax is not the only public policy that has redistributive effects. There is nothing sacred about maintaining federal income tax revenue. A redistribution of tax burden from income to consumption is perfectly feasible. But these are separate issues. Federal personal exemptions should be closely related to minimum living costs; that means to the minimum wage. They are not.

The income tax is much less progressive that it seems on the basis of brackets and rates, and much less fair. A progressive income tax which indirectly redistributes income from the richer to the poorer is almost universally accepted. But except for the marginal tax rates, its current tax provisions benefit the higher income and asset-rich taxpayers much more than taxpayers lower in income brackets, and asset-poor. The individual income tax is intended to raise revenue to pay for the functions of government. But as a means of reducing income inequality; ours is not up to the job. It should not be subverted into a device for special privilege or social engineering as it is now.

Chapter 16

WHEN SOLUTIONS ARE THE PROBLEM

Currencies collapse, countries hover on the edge of bankruptcy, people riot in the streets against all solutions. Many despair at the intractable problems of our times. But which are the problems, which the solutions, and are they really intractable? I suggest that there are only two 24 carat problems: deficits, which are short run historically speaking, and environmental degradation, which is longer term. If one regards climate as a problem, it is the only one that is insoluble. All the other problems are also solutions. Most of the solutions are also problems in their own right or create problems. No wonder some despair.

Which is worse, the problem or the solution? In any case one must address this puzzle nation by nation, since circumstances, perspectives and correctives differ widely. Most of the intractable problems are soluble, but most of the solutions are beyond the authority or power of the state. So government officials should despair, but citizens need not.

Reducing and terminating environment degradation requires a large decline in population and a decline in levels of living. Most nations outside of Africa, all over100 million population except Pakistan, have fertility rates at or below replacement. All East Asian nations have fertility well below China's without any public policy. World population is on its way to decline.

This solution generates another major problem: declining ratio of workers to population, which means declining levels of living for most countries. Lower levels of living in turn mean reduced pressure on natural resources and the environment, another part of solution of the environmental degradation problem. The rising dependency ratio increases the problem of over-commitment on pensions and other entitlements, worsens the prospect of reducing the deficit. There are fewer workers, lower incomes, and more entitlement recipients. Thus less affluence is both a problem and a solution.

The U.S. dependency ratio increase may be temporary; the retirement of the baby boom generation; not so most other countries. Our solution to social security bankruptcy is easy: raising working age to 70 will do most of the job. This is the one solution that is not also a problem, at least in the United States, a workaholic society. In most of Europe it is seen more as a problem, an additional burden, than a solution. Other countries will have greater difficulty increasing working age, or hours of work, and their entitlement burdens are greater than ours because of higher dependency ratios.

Forget climate. Problem or not, there is nothing we can do about it this century. Canada and Russia will be great beneficiaries of warming, they will not sacrifice. The US is a small beneficiary as well. China, India, Brazil place growth first, second and third. Besides, the solution is worse than the problem. The cost of a minute reduction in temperature greatly exceeds any potential benefits. Cutting our standard of living back 100 years will have imperceptible outcomes. The cost of adapting to temperature change is much lower. Improve energy efficiency by all means, and reduce energy use. But sun power costs much more than gas and there is no prospect of it being competitive in the near future, nor can it account for more than a small fraction of our needs unless we learn to store it for up to 6 months cheaply or transfer it across hemispheres in volume cheaply.

My gut feeling is that we should focus on the intractable problems that are not themselves solutions: deficit and environment, opting for solutions that minimize exacerbation of other problems. No tunnel vision please.

The current problems can only get worse if not confronted. How can we engender the required focus, discipline, sacrifice? There is a familiar way: Nothing would work better than a nasty war. We may be testing this hypothesis in the near future. But that is a solution that is worse than the deficit problem, and aggravates our environmental woes.

Perhaps despair is not so much over the economic/demographic, environmental problems mentioned above, but about issues of human life and liberty: war and human rights. On that I despair. Civilization is a permanent struggle against human nature. Homo Credens must be surpassed.

Chapter 17

NO GOOD DEED SHALL GO UNPUNISHED

This is not a diatribe against compassion, but a plea for cognition. Often our efforts to help the poor, the disadvantaged do more harm than good. Always there are unintended consequences, which if considered in advance, lead to more intelligent and effective policy.

THE PREVALENCE OF UNINTENDED CONSEQUENCES

We know from past experience that welfare programs can discourage initiative to search for work, to improve labor market skills. Unemployment compensation can be too generous or prolonged, again discouraging search for work or raising reservation wages too high. These are predictable consequences, although their magnitude is debatable.

Next consider efforts to improve the environment. Restrictions on drilling for oil offshore and in onshore federal lands have on one hand promoted deep sea drilling, much more expensive, much riskier, and a much greater threat to the environment, as we learned with the BP oil spill. Onshore, we have created demand and supply of the dirtiest available oil whose extraction does the greatest damage to the environment, which generates more carbon dioxide that would the prohibited sources: the Canadian tar sands oil industry. Now it is promoting another highly damaging industry in the United States: shale oil extraction. The refusal to allow a pipeline to be built carrying tar sands oil from Canada to Texas refineries simply means that refineries should be built in Canada. We will still import tar sands oil, but already refined, and will have to compete with Japan and China for supply.,Subsidies for domestic production of ethanol from corn and requirements that it be added to motor vehicle fuel have increased food prices throughout the world, counteracting our efforts to allay malnutrition and reduce poverty in less developed countries. It is not clear that production and use of ethanol reduces CO2 emissions.

Efforts to promote health by indiscriminate testing for prostate cancer and breast cancer have increased costs, anxiety, without perceptible effect on life expectancy. The focus on treatment for AIDS to the neglect of prevention have not cured HIV-positive individuals but have prolonged their lives, the net result is an increased number of infections, as HIV-positive individuals have more sexual contacts with more individuals over a longer period of time. Less expensive efforts at prevention would have reduced infections instead of increasing them.

Foreign aid is not an unmitigated blessing. Sanitation, vaccination, public health have greatly accelerated population growth. In some parts of the world they have increased the number of poor people. But this consequence is avoidable.

. The population explosion itself is one of two primary causes of increases in CO2 emissions; the other is increasing affluence Population growth and rising incomes are the dominant causes of environmental degradation and depletion of renewable resources as well as rising prices and accelerated exhaustion of minerals and fossil fuels. This is not an argument against aid or affluence, just a reminder that good intentions can have unwanted consequences.

THE FALLACY OF COMPOSITION

Some unintended consequences are not only predictable, they may be comparable since they refer to a common objective. The principle of composition refers to a scale effect. The outcome of a choice depends on how many people make the same choice. If I buy or sell 100 shares of corporation X, share prices are unaffected. But if a large number of people do as I do, prices will rise or fall. If I get a college degree, the supply of college graduates is increased so little that job prospects and pay are unaffected. But if an additional million people graduate this year, the outcome will be quite different.

College for all is the main current case of individual benefits but collective loss. Any one, or a few, individuals, will be better off going to college than stopping with high school graduation, but if almost everyone goes to college, and forty percent of an age group graduate, the degree is no longer selective, prestigious, and the jobs available for most graduates are much less attractive than those available when few went to college.

The scale effect t from the perspective of the nation is not the same as that of the individual. If everyone goes to college the labor force is more productive, the political system may be more efficient, society may be fairer. But working years are reduced, income is diverted from consumption and investment to education. There are a lot of maybes.

The current example, which may persist for a generation, is the housing crisis. A good deed it was not, but there was no evil intent. Banks offered home mortgages to lenders whose probability of payment was low. They reasoned that, should the borrowers default, the foreclosed houses could be sold at prices higher than the mortgage. House prices were rising, and expectations were for a continued increase. The reasoning was sound for any one bank, any one loan, but when many banks made many high-risk loans, the number of failed mortgages, of foreclosed houses on the market rose to the point that housing prices fell. Soon enough prices fell below the amount of the mortgage unpaid for millions of home buyers, and banks were in trouble.

The fallacy of composition is also one foundation of unintended consequences. Honesty is the best policy if everyone is honest; not necessarily for a particular individual otherwise. Taxes are lower if everyone pays taxes according to the law. No security systems are needed if no one steals.

Unintended consequences may be far in the future, or to someone else, or just very difficult to estimate, much less measure or compare with the intended outcomes of a public policy. Mortals discount the future, the remote. Thus they are not always considered, never given full weight. They complicate decision-making and weaken support whenever they are seen as negative, inflate support when seen as positive.

Tunnel vision is what we want, single minded focus, when we know what the problem is and exactly how to deal with it. But identifying the problem, and selecting appropriate solutions requires wide angle vision.

Chapter 18

IS DEMOCRACY A PONZI SCHEME?

Our original democracy was individual, with just three entitlements: life, liberty, and pursuit of happiness. All democracy today is social. Government is about security and redistribution. The State is involved in public education, unemployment compensation/welfare, health care, retirement income. The last two redistribute income from the working generation to older generations. Education redistributes to the young.

INTER-GENERATIONAL TRANSFERS

Transfers from workers to the next generation prepare children to take their turn in supporting their elders. The costs have increased because educational attainment has risen. In the past 50 years the proportion of college graduates in the work force has quadrupled. Furthermore, prices have risen for college education. These inter-generational transfers are not one-sided. The young repay their elders in later years for their past contributions. This system of reciprocal subsidies works well much of the time, as long as each new generation is larger and/or wealthier than its predecessor, and oldsters do not experience large gains in longevity. These requirements of a successful PONZI scheme prevailed in the past but have broken down.

The baby boomers were almost twice as numerous as their predecessor, but succeeding generations were smaller. Median earnings have not risen in recent decades, and are now declining. Meanwhile, health care costs and retirement income needs for the aged have risen, as their numbers grow more rapidly than the labor force. Longevity is a burden. Successive generations are unable or unwilling to bear the burden. The system is bankrupt.

Demographic Revolution

Why do not the elderly provide for their retirement years during their working life? Social Security and Medicare were conceived as insurance policies, paid in advance via the payroll; tax. Social Security contributions and payments were determined by past income, with redistribution a function of differences in longevity. Medicare was health insurance, with reimbursement based on individual health care needs and contributions based on income.

Social Security pensions and medical reimbursements have forged ahead of contributions. Their funding via a payroll tax did not anticipate a large increase in longevity among the 65-plus population. An additional failure of foresight was the high cost of new health care medications and procedures.

The Social Security payroll tax started at 2% in 1937, rose rapidly to 12.4% in 1994, remaining unchanged until 2011. The Medicare payroll tax started at 0.7% in 1966, rising rapidly to 2.9% in 1986, where it remains today. The revenues are already quite insufficient to cover the cost of benefits, and becoming more so as the ratio of elderly to working age population keeps rising. But there is adamant resistance to cuts in benefits or increases in taxes. The reckoning was delayed by the increase in labor force participation of women, but no more. Payroll taxes high enough to finance future costs of current entitlements would be counter-productive in any case; they would diminish investment and economic growth. By the time Medicare was enacted demographers already knew that the population 65 and older was bound to increase rapidly after 2010 with the retirement of the baby boom generation. Longevity increases were already outpacing their projections as penicillin cut pneumonia death rates among the elderly. Presidents and politicians have known for several decades that the system of inter-generational transfers was unsustainable. But they underestimated the increase in health care costs, and perhaps in longevity as well.

Negative Sum Games

As long as the working population is increasing in numbers and/or in earnings faster that the growth of population 65 and older, it is possible to increase benefits to the elderly without raising tax rates; or to maintain benefits and lower tax rates. This is a positive sum game. There is an incentive to compromise since both parties gain. But if the number of benefit recipients is growing faster than worker earnings, then maintaining benefit levels requires a rise in tax rates, or a cut in benefits is required to avoid raising tax rates. This is a negative sum game; with loss to both sides; there is no incentive to play. The longer that adjustment in the system is delayed, the larger is the total loss to be distributed, hence the more difficult to come to any agreement.

Is democracy possible when demography and/or economy dictate that redistribution is a negative sum game? At this time in many democratic nations, the obligations of social democracy exceed the resources of the state, and appear to exceed the willingness and ability of workers to pay. There are also adverse unintended consequences on economic growth of efforts to raise the revenues required to fulfill statutory obligations.

With the economy growing and per capita incomes rising, inter-generational income distribution is a positive sum game. National priorities are growth, not distribution. But once incomes are no longer rising, the gain of one group is at the expense of another group. Distribution becomes the central bone of contention. Inequality of labor income is only one way of expressing the issue: class warfare. Financing the pensions and health care of the elderly by taxation of workers is another perspective: generational warfare.

Very little has been done about Social Security - a slow and limited increase in retirement age. And nothing systematic has been done about increasing deficits for Medicare. Social security recipients oppose benefit cuts, and payroll taxpayers oppose tax increases. Medicare patients do not reduce their demand, nor do their physicians restrict their supply of prescriptions, procedures. Changes in the structure of health care delivery are widely opposed. Citizens are partisan; they vote their interests. Can we expect their representatives to vote for the national interest? Deficits inflate interest payments, curtailing other government expenditures. Default clears the deck of past debt; it cannot deal with deficits and debt continuing in the future. It is a means of defrauding lenders, but will also penalize everyone else by reducing the value of their currency. It precludes further deficits; who will lend to such a borrower? It can default by inflation.

Can governments borrow to fulfill obligations ? Yes, but not for long. Small nations whose debt is held mainly by foreigners can out-source the costs of default and forget about future borrowing. A large nation much of whose government debt is held at home simply robs its own citizens.

There are two obstacles to rational decision-making in the public interest in a democracy. The first is the commons: most of the benefit of a good decision, most of the harm of a bad decision, accrue to others. The requirement for good decisions is sainthood: counting all costs and benefits without regard to whom they accrue.

The other problem is the undervaluation of the future and the time horizon. For individuals, the maximum time horizon is the expected remaining life span unless they incorporate the costs and benefits of survivors after their own death. For many if not most politicians, the horizon is the next election. Thus the requirement for rational decision-making in this case is authoritarianism. Rare is the president or congressman who ignores reelection in decision-making.

The only instances in which a democracy has managed an orderly and accepted decline in income has been wartime. It is a period of command and control. The distribution ordained was the drafting of men and of the economy, egalitarian: rationing of critical commodities, the same for rich and poor; a top marginal income tax rate of 93% in the United States. The surplus thus generated goes to war. But war is not a solution for a negative sum game; it is the game. If a nation cannot reach a consensus on sharing losses, global consensus on issues such as climate policy are impossible.

Splitting the difference is an egalitarian analogy to war rationing, but it is just a delaying tactic. Entitlements must be reconsidered: age of eligibility, benefit packages, co-payments. In the case of health care, entitlement limits need to be set. Can it be done in peacetime? Is democracy a fair weather system, a PONZI plot doomed by demography? Or is it inevitably afflicted by myopia and tunnel vision?

Democracy is particularly ill-suited for compromises when the losses are considerable and long-lasting. The alternative, representative authoritarianism, is undesirable not because it cannot accomplish the task but because it is unlikely to limit its authority or duration to its assigned purpose.

The division of labor between public and private, between collective and individual initiative and responsibility, is a matter of choice. Some issues can be exempt from the political process and the need for agreement. Democracy is consensual in handling scalable issues, since compromise is possible. It is combative in deciding binary choices between mutually exclusive alternatives. But when there is need to share losses, democracy is on trial.

In wartime there is a shared objective. Democracies, based on popular authority and its delegation, have instituted war powers, which are top-down authority: the draft of people and the economy. It has worked because there was a common objective. Once the objective was achieved, or no longer shared. authority reverted to the people, bottom up. The current and future crises are not about life and death, but affluence and poverty, employment and unemployment. Is there some point, whether deficit, debt, interest payments on the debt, at which people come to share an objective and are willing to divest their authority to leaders until the crisis is solved, or must there be default, and chaotic devaluation for everyone? Much depends on the culture rather than on the political structure. A communitarian culture is more likely to share policy objectives and goals than an individualistic culture. It is more prone to share losses. This is also true of an egalitarian culture, itself likely to be communal. But community may mean just family, really individualism extended, or class, ethnicity, or other grouping, or encompass almost the entire nation, as in Japan, perhaps therefore the nation best positioned to deal with the crisis. American individualism is not just egocentrism, it is mellowed by a concern for others, the community, the environment. So there is hope. however faint.

Democracy was a by-product of the struggle against autocracy. It was designed to be weak; the state was the servant of society; the executive was constrained by the congress and judiciary, all limited in choices by a constitution.

Diversity, not democracy, is the cause of failure. It is a matter of culture. A crisis calls for a common purpose, united effort. If it is external: war or natural disaster, democracy can cope. But if it is internal: conflict of policy with reality, conflict of interests, goals, democracy seems helpless.

A negative sum game requires discipline. Austerity is rarely self-imposed. It is easier in northern Europe, whose culture is "Life, Order and Equality" than in the United States, which recognizes the conflict between liberty and equality, and is less concerned with order. Crisis calls for elevation of order and equality above liberty, a brief suspension of national culture.

We do not wish to abandon democracy. But its structure needs amendment to provide for crisis management. The need is temporary. Could it be met by one of the existing branches of government? The executive is appropriate for crises of subsistence or survival: external crises. But there are crises of identity and belief, such as we witness in the Muslim world. These are internal. The crisis of the advanced nations is a conflict of interests and goals, not an executive responsibility. There must be a temporary change in the structure of decision making, whether by legislative authority, or constitutional amendment.

Chapter 19

DEMOCRACY AND RELIGION

Authority has two dimensions: vertical and horizontal. Vertical authority may be top down, which we call dictatorship, or bottom up, which we call democracy. The horizontal dimension refers to the range over which authority can be exercised. If vast or unlimited, we call it totalitarianism if top down, anarchy if bottom up. If the range is small, call it limited government. Limited governments may coexist with a number of private authorities with specific jurisdictions, including churches.

Democracy encompasses a wide range of institutional arrangements. At one extreme is the referendum, direct democracy, no representation, no delegation. This is workable for decisions on single issues, and as a means of authorizing a constitution, but no way to run any organization. As a practicable institution, at one extreme democracy involves direct election of president, legislature, and judiciary. These three separate branches of government are an essential condition. They represent division of labor that avoids conflicts of interest and monopoly of power between elections. They also function in different time frames. Executive policies are daily activities of an electoral cycle; laws are for an indefinite future but subject to change; justice is timeless. Partial democracy involves some delegation: voters choose governors, who choose the president; or elect the legislature, which selects the president, or voters elect a president who appoints governors, they delegate judiciary selection to one or more of the above. Democratic government is government for all the people, not just for those who elected it and it is subordinate to the law of the land, which must be constitutional.

There is much more to democracy than the form, the institutions, the process. It is about human rights, about culture. People must understand that they help influence public decisions, but do not necessarily get their way. And democracy is not just for men, or for particular ethnicities or races. Rejection of top down authority is not democracy, it could be simple anarchy. Voting is not enough; there must be individualism; the voter should be independent of clan, tribe, caste, class, ethnicity. It does not flourish in a hierarchical society. There are cultural requirements that many nations cannot meet.

A church as an institution may be democratic in any of the forms indicated above, but have different branches of government such as missionary work, training for the ministry. Church and state can coexist, but a democracy must be secular. The conflict between religion and democracy may be one of competition for authority: church laws, courts, financial obligations. It is the institution, not the faith, that can be in conflict. The authority of a church extends only to those who choose to be members, and it cannot conflict with the state. It may propose higher standards of behavior, but not impose them, nor authorize behavior forbidden by the state.

More common is a conflict of culture. Religion is authoritarian; it is the ultimate authority. God does not run for reelection, the commandments are not subject to amendment or annulment. The universe is not of our doing. In some faiths believers bow only to God; in others they prostrate themselves at every step up the ladder of hierarchical authority. It is the culture of authority and obedience that is incompatible with representative democracy. One is top down authority, delegation, the other is bottom up authority, representation. It is much to expect most individuals to behave in one manner in civil society, and in a radically different manner in the religious community: that is schizophrenia. I leave it to historians to decide to what extent culture shapes faith, or faith influences culture.

But religions differ in authority structure. Christians believe in free will; the individual is responsible for his behavior, has a conscience, a sense of guilt. Islam believes that Allah makes all decisions, Allah is a micromanager. Hence the individual has a weak sense of responsibility for his behavior, little sense of guilt, an underdeveloped conscience. As to the range of authority, Christianity has arrived at a separation between church and state, the sacred and the secular. Islam recognizes no such division. The sacred rules over all. Hence again in the former there is a wide range of individual autonomy and responsibility, in the latter there is ultimately none.

Religions and their institutions differ in their requirements of believers. Confucianism is not a religion but the closest approach to one for most Chinese. He taught good manners, proper behavior in the family, in particular deference to one's ancestors. But his teachings were soon extended by analogy to the nation, with the Emperor as father. In fact Confucius provided an ethical veneer for what Wittfogel called "Oriental Despotism". The Emperor is godlike, subject to no law, his word is law. His children listen, memorize, obey; they never question. Mao was the last Emperor, China is now ruled by a committee of ten little emperors. Such behavior, such a culture, is incompatible with democracy, in which diverse views, disagreements are part of the decision-making process which involves all citizens, not just the Emperor's court.

The same is true of Islam, and its holy book, the Koran, not one word of which can be changed, but all words should be memorized. The first commandment is obedience. Worship is prostration. Islam has a further burden in a democratic society: it is not ecumenical. Believers and unbelievers are subject to different ethical rules. Apostates in particular are beyond the moral world. This is not to say that Christians have not at times behaved in the same way, but such behavior is contrary to Christian teaching, which is ecumenical, the same ethics for believers and unbelievers, for all peoples.

It is possible for many individuals to live in two worlds, inquiring and argumentative in the secular world, participating in decision making; unquestioning and obedient in the sacred world. But there is always the imperative temptation, the desire to extend the boundaries of the sacred into secular territory: its own practices, laws, courts, bureaucracy. Such temptation may be inherent in the religion, or simply the ambition of bureaucracy. This urge is just as true of the secular religions. It is seen as missionary work by some, holy imperialism by others. Democracy is never safe.

Chapter 20

NATIONAL IDENTITY, NATIONAL GOALS

EXCEPTIONALISM

America is the exceptional nation. In the twentieth century it was also the indispensable nation. There are diverse views on what is exceptional. To my mind the most important is that this is the one nation whose identity is ideological. By implication, it is an identity free of ethnic or historical attributes, although its history reflects its ideology. It is simply summarized by Thomas Jefferson, "Life, Liberty and Pursuit of Happiness," sequential values each dependent on its predecessor. Other nations have values, although they are not the source of their identity. The French "Liberté, Egalité, Fraternité is a slogan of the French Revolution, not a replacement for ethnic identity. European nations may prefer "Life, Order, and Equality". Liberty is important, but not at the sacrifice of order or as promoter of inequality. Different values, different cultures, different histories.

It was exceptional until recently in another way: an incredible rate of population growth, from under 2.5 million in 1776 to 309 in 2010. It is no longer so exceptional in this regard, its growth rate has slowed. But its ideological identity made it welcome immigrants as few other countries ever did.

A third characteristic is that America, unlike many European nations and Japan, never sought to become a colonial power and refused the opportunity. It inherited Spanish colonies in the Caribbean and the Philippines after the war of 1898, but liberated some immediately and proceeded to prepare the others for self-government and independence. This represented an extension of its ideology to other peoples, nations. After WWII it refused the request of numerous Pacific islands for incorporation in the United States, but assumed some responsibility for their development and protection, another extension of its ideology beyond its borders.

Its imperialism was also unique (apart from the demographic imperialism across a thinly populated semi-continent) it was world-wide, not focused on particular lands. It consisted of aid and technical assistance for economic development and missionary efforts in behalf of human rights: cost, not revenue.

The fourth aspect of exceptionalism, also following from its ideological identity, can be called messiahnism. Starting with the colonies inherited from Spain, but especially following WWI, it sought to export democracy under the delusion that it embodied its ideals. In fact democracy could embody a somewhat different set or sequence of ideals, in nations whose values or priorities were different from ours. This ideological export remains an American priority. But in recent decades it has sought to promote "human rights" in other nations. It is a means of promoting its ideology even in, especially in, nations that do not allow or accept democracy.

A Moment in History

Woodrow Wilson dreamed of a peaceful and democratic world, after WWI, but the victors were not ready, neither was the United States. America was not yet a dominant power. After WWII America was dominant, and sought to shape a better world through economic growth leading to freedom and democracy. The UN was to be the political institution; the World Bank would promote growth, and the IMF, stability. The World Bank had some successes, but overall it failed, as did the expectation that economic growth assured freedom, human rights, democracy. The UN proved ineffective. The stress on universal membership sacrificed coherence and credibility. It was a very brief moment of opportunity, terminated by the Berlin airlift and the Korean proxy war. The struggle to contain an aggressive Soviet Union diverted American efforts and attention.

America built its own institutions committed to aid underdeveloped nations, which persist today. The examples had consequences: other regional international development banks were established; other nations, once they had recovered from the war, also established their own international aid and development institutions. So did some nations, former recipients of aid, once they became affluent. It was a vision and the world is better for it despite its failings.

Shortly after WWII Americans invested in their own future as well: free college education for veterans, a national highway system, the entry of most women in the labor force, the second emancipation of African-Americans, a vast research and development effort, then computers and the internet, new systems of information and communication open to all. It created its own history.

The future is now. What next? The taste for novelty is still there, in which America is exceptional but not unique. Savings and investment are down, research and development are neglected, the quality of education is low and not well directed toward the needs of the future.

Democracy is said to function only in the short run. Politicians' time horizon is the next election. Since voters have an insatiable demand for public services and benefits but great reluctance to pay for them, politicians oblige via bigger government and growing debt. The natural behavior of a democratic politician is not always in the national interest. Once the nation thought long term, planned and spent for a better world. It sought to make history. But that was a heroic time. Now we react, we seek to predict, not to shape the future.

The moment when America made history will not return. America did serve until recently as policeman of the world, preventing numerous conflicts, ending a few, but that role is now over. It lacks the will, the credibility, and soon will lack the capacity.

It still serves as a model for much of the world, a promised land of what the future can be, freedom, opportunity, affluence, creativity. Perhaps that is enough. It is a model because of its continental scale, its global reach, its history. Other nations have outperformed it in any particular achievement, but they lack the power. Above all it is the one nation whose identity is ideological, unifying, whereas most others are ethnic in identity, separatist. The world will watch how it manages the unintended consequences of its own and others' achievements: longevity, entitlements, stagnation.

America does think long term in terms of the search for knowledge, the search for scientific solutions. One needs to distinguish between research projects and programs, agendas. Projects tend to be short term: they succeed or fail. The search for a malaria vaccine is very long term because it has failed. This is also true of the billions of dollars spent over half a century on nuclear fusion. The War on Cancer initiated by L.B. Johnson goes on, some successes, many failures. The National Institutes of Health, the National Science Foundation, NASA are long term programs by their institutionalized nature. But they depend on taxpayer support. So is agricultural research not only by the Department of Agriculture, but in the land grant universities. But perhaps the most far-sighted research program is, has been, the Defense Department. We only learn about some of its projects long after the fact. Defense research has been the main contributor to scientific/technical progress in the last 80 years.

Only research can give us the means of responding to the challenges we are confronting today, but it will not give us the will. What is lacking is an overarching vision for society as a whole. "More is better" is not much of a vision. Perhaps it is too much to expect from a nation whose very name is plural.

The United States has been unwilling to stop the development of nuclear weapons in several countries. Now it waits in hope of a transformation in China and Russia, leaving Islamic terrorism as the main remaining international threat. These were problems which America could tackle, and only America, with international cooperation. The problems of the future require international if not global cooperation: depletion of renewable resources such as ocean fisheries, forests, disease control, cooperation on climate, terrorism. They are beyond the reach of power and wealth alone. In the era of information and communication, America must provide example and persuasion. Who else? It is the future-oriented nation.

Chapter 21

POPULATION BUST

Many know that Russia and Japan are declining in population. Few realize that nearly all advanced nations will be following suit. Replacement fertility is 2.1 children per woman in countries with low infant, child and maternal mortality and roughly equal numbers of males and females, considerably higher in countries that don't meet these conditions.

Fertility rates are falling across the world. They are below replacement in nearly all advanced nations, currently including the United States, whose growth in recent years has been thanks to immigrants. They are far below replacement for Germany, southern Europe. Fertility rates for the largest Latin American countries: Brazil, Mexico, Colombia and Argentina, are at or below replacement level. Only a few nations with small populations have fertility rates above replacement. There is a similar decline of fertility in Muslim countries. Among large countries only Pakistan has a fertility rate well above replacement, Indonesia, Bangladesh, Turkey and Iran are at or below replacement. All East Asia has fertility rates far below replacement. In South Asia, India is the main exception for the time being, but its rate is only slightly above replacement. Most of Africa still has fertility rates far above replacement, but they are falling. South Africa's' Lesotho's and Botswana's are not much above replacement.

Why this sudden worldwide decline in fertility? The motivation to reduce child-bearing has exploded. Urbanization, and compulsory schooling, make children an economic burden into their teens. The exposure to the life styles of the middle and upper classes through the revolution in information and communication change aspirations. The consumer culture values acquisition of material goods and personal indulgence above the burdens and blessings of child rearing. The liberation of women, their increased participation in the labor force is also a factor.

Now there are means of restricting fertility not available in the past: the pill, condoms, imaging when there is a strong sex preference, and greater acceptance of abortion. These changes are irreversible. It is possible that many countries with a very low fertility rate will experience an increase in the ratio of males to female births, as China has, worsening the consequences of low fertility and creating additional problems.

What are the consequences? As each new generation is smaller than its predecessor, first the labor force begins to shrink. Second, the dependency ratio begins to rise, as generations achieving retirement age are always larger than those entering the labor force. (Dependency is defined as population under 15 plus over 65 divided by population 15-65.) Early on, population begins to decline. The rising ratio of non-workers to workers means a decline in growth rates in income per capita, possibly a continual decline in levels of living for most nations. Eventually scale economies in production and distribution diminish, and costs of living rise.

All three trends will lead many nations declining in population ro seek immigrants to increase their labor force, and reduce their dependency ratio. Most will become reluctant to see any of their people leave. There will be international disputes, if not conflict, between nations whose young workers are emigrating and nations that are accepting them. Nations whose borders have been changed in recent history may seek to recover their populations lost in the process. But migration policies merely redistribute shortages in labor force, a decline in population, and a rise in the dependency ratio

This is a new historical experience. We don't know the outcome, but we can conceive of three scenarios: 1. The last human on earth will be the son of an Orthodox rabbi on the West Bank around the 2900s. 2. As population density falls below the level required to preserve urbanization and industrial production, humans will return to subsistence farming, perhaps to hunting and gathering as forests and fisheries rebound. 3. Some primitive tribe. never in contact with civilization, in the Amazon or New Guinea, will survive and multiply, discover the abandoned cities, loot them, unable to puzzle what to do with much of what they find, and create a new legend of a lost Atlantis and perhaps a superior race of beings.

Humanity will not become an endangered species without a struggle. Financial incentives, such as doubling the personal income tax exemption for dependent children, will fail. We know already that those best able to bear the economic burden of raising children are the ones least likely to have children.

Policies toward birth control and abortion will be reconsidered. Some nations will seek to ban the production, sale, and ownership of all birth control means. They will censor information on the subject, hoping to restart the whole process of overpopulation. They depend on the male sex drive. reinforced by food additives.

Child bearing and child rearing will be separated. Some women will make a living bearing and carrying to term the progeny of others, but surrogate, mothers are few and costly. Bioengineers may develop artificial wombs to shelter and nurture fetuses to term. Child rearing will be facilitated by the state. Child care centers, pre-kindergartens are nothing new, nor orphanages and boarding houses. But psychologists will worry about the socialization of a nation of orphans.

Other nations will follow the example of China, which will convert its abortion clinics into fertility factories, and may require that all women over 30 who have not produced children be impregnated according to the law. Eugenics and national survival will be combined in the Population Plan. The Genghis Khan model of Propagator in Chief worked too slowly, so a new class of civil servants will be selected for the task by examination and a fee.

There is a way of ending or reversing the trend of depopulation less authoritarian than the compulsory impregnation of childless women. Child bearing and rearing can be industrialized. Adults will still contribute the seeds of life, but they will sprout in artificial wombs. Their identity will be a closely guarded state secret. Babies will grow to maturity on factory farms. They will grow up like puppies, wagging their tails at food machines and their adult caretakers, mainly women with insatiable maternal instincts, but still a generation of orphans. This is a close approximation to George Bernard Shaw's recommendation that humans become oviparous and hatch at age 17.

Nearly all households will be adults only. Paternal, maternal, and filial relations will be very rare. Society must reinvent social bonds, since it will be populated by orphans. Sex ratios will still matter, but only to promote egalitarianism in recreation.

There will be a residual community of narcissists dedicated to perpetuate their genetic identity. But few will choose this costly way of reproduction and child rearing.

Nations that adopt the factory system will populate the world, like the early farmers who displaced the hunter-gatherers through their higher fertility and survival. Population will be national and international policy, not individual choice. Eugenics will become practicable and possibly the main issue of public dispute. There may be population wars. Ovum and sperm banks would be prime targets.

Perhaps decline is better than the Malthusian trap. If humans do not want progeny, they have lost a sense of the future. Let them become an endangered species.

Chapter 22

SHRINKING CITIES: ADAPTING TO POPULATION DECLINE

World population quadrupled in the 20th century. But population did not grow everywhere. In the more developed countries rural population declined in many regions as people moved to cities. In some countries with high population density, villages and small towns shrank in size, In others, such as the United States, many villages and small towns were abandoned. But this process was driven by economic growth, job opportunities, as well as quality of life in cities, and productivity gains in agriculture.

As low-skill labor-intensive industries moved within nations and then emigrated to nations with low labor costs, some large cities lost population. This was true of the textile and apparel industry in the United States. Later, other industries dependent on raw materials shifted location and nationality as their resource supplies became exhausted or costly. The metals industries are a case in point. Lower trade barriers and lower transport costs also played a role in these inter-regional and international shifts in location of production. Big cities: Pittsburgh, Detroit, Baltimore, St. Louis lost population. But recovery was a reasonable expectation at a time when national population was growing, as new industries were created and new firms established.

The situation is quite different when the primary cause of population decline in large cities is national population decline. New industries may still arise, and new companies founded, some old ones may expand, but labor force and employment are declining. A gain by one city, or even stability, implies loss, decline of other cities. What was once a positive sum game has turned negative nationally and internationally.

How shall a large city respond to large and growing numbers of abandoned houses and other urban structures? In the past such abandonments were concentrated near urban centers as population suburbanized. In the future, abandoned structures are likely to be found throughout an urban area. We know that abandoned houses attract vermin, both animal and human. How should cities facing permanent decline deal with this situation?

There is a further problem,. City services designed for a larger population are now under-utilized. How can a city with declining tax base maintain services such as transportation and utilities, or hospitals with a large capital component which are city-wide, unlike schools, whose service areas are flexible and not city-wide and whose services are not capital-intensive? The more a city shrinks in population, the higher the cost of such public services, whether they are government or privately owned. An initial decline could become a downward spiral. Detroit has declared bankruptcy.

One approach to minimize costs of population decline is investment in mobile homes. I am not suggesting conversion of cities into trailer parks. Some 5 percent of new houses are factory-made and assembled on a local foundation. They can be moved to another foundation. City government can relocate them as part of its downsizing policy, they can replace houses abandoned and razed in areas selected for preservation. The owners avoid the loss of value and the risks of remaining in a depopulating neighborhood. They would leave behind an empty lot, not an abandoned house.

The predominance of one and two person households suggests replacement of the detached family house ideal and the restructuring of cities into apartment complexes with centralized facilities for heating, cooling, laundry, garbage. Such a model requires much less space per capita, releasing land for parks, urban farming, urban forest. As insurance against depopulation, families should not regard housing as a multigenerational investment. The home rental market should grow at the expense of home ownership.

There is another prospect affecting all advanced nations, whatever their population trends. This is the prevalence of remote communication and availability of remote control. Many people will work at home, there is much less need for work space outside the home. Many activities, processes can be controlled remotely. More work is performed by robots, there is some reduction in work space as well; robots do not need restrooms or bedding. In either case there is reduced need for work space outside the home.

From the consumer viewpoint, many stores are no longer necessary. The consumer can order most items on his shopping list on the web. Stores are replaced by warehouses, with great savings in space. And these can be in another city or in the countryside. Urban planners and builders must consider what functions, facilities, services require physical presence, and which of these should be locally accessible, which centrally. Swimming pools and playgrounds are neighborhood, restaurants are both, so are medical facilities. Most government and highly specialized services are city-wide, best located near the center. Shopping centers could become a wave of the past, the home delivery services a growth industry.

Urban reorganization faces a difficult period of transition, as tax base shrinks but the cost of urban infrastructure in place does not. Infrastructure planning for the future becomes riskier, as the traditional expectation that a city would not decline but would almost surely grow must be abandoned.

The United States does not face the prospect of population decline in the immediate future since its pre-recession fertility rate was close to replacement levels and the gap was filled by immigrants. But Japan and Europe will begin to face it this decade. It is a gradual process. But working out solutions should start soon. A city through its policies for infrastructure and services can influence the areas that will be abandoned and those that will be preserved. City limits may be constricted, zones depopulated. That also means that city government can determine who will lose much, who will lose little or nothing, who may be displaced. The mere announcement of plans will affect property values. This is a nearly intractable political issue. But allowing decay and depopulation to proceed without any direction also affects some areas more than others. Since city governments must respond to the consequences of market forces in any case, it may be wise to influence those forces to reduce the unintended consequences - the neighborhood effects of depopulation.

Even the United States must confront the consequences of the information age for work space, for shopping and service space. The depressed neighborhoods of the future could be commercial, not residential. The empty storefronts which we associate with the current recession may never be filled again.

Chapter 23

The Right to Emigrate

This is a nation of immigrants. The huddled masses sailing from Europe in the 19th and early 20th centuries represented gains for all countries concerned. They came to a subcontinent with empty land, a need for workers, from nations with agricultural overpopulation, beginning to lose manufacturing jobs to other continents. Since then there have been changes in immigrant origin and characteristics and US population and need for workers. The costs and benefits of migration have changed. The main aspects of current and future migration may be characterized as brain flows, fiscal flows and population flows.

Education and Brain Drain

The United States is the world's greatest recipient of foreign aid, much of it from low-income nations. It is not cash, but brains: scientists, engineers, computer specialists, MDs. Should the emigrants reimburse their governments for the costs of their education? Or should our government assume this responsibility? It would be a tariff on brain imports.

The flow of immigrants until the early twentieth century was not foreign aid. It was not a transfer of human capital, only of potential, There has always been a trickle of brains, but the great brain flow, starting shortly before WWII, is a different story - a loss to the country of origin, gain to the United States. For us it is a bargain, since education is more expensive here than in almost any other nation. Such immigrants are a major source of invention that keeps our economy moving forward. Their entry should be encouraged. The fact that it is highly restricted may be in the interest of professional groups who shun competition, but to no one else's benefit.

Fiscal Flows: Remittances and Retirement

The balance of benefits and costs is different for the much larger flows in recent decades of immigrants lacking education or skills. The first issue is immigrant remittances, benefit for the home country, but income not spent and providing employment in the country where they live. A more important issue is of recent origin: Medicaid, welfare, unemployment compensation and other programs in behalf of the poor. Immigrant need for these benefits is well above the average. Demand depends on legal status; an illegal alien is less likely to seek aid than others with equal needs. As to supply, public education is an investment, hence should be available to illegal immigrants. Public subsidies for medical care cannot be so easily categorized. Welfare programs are simply redistributive.

The third issue is largely in the future. How many immigrants on retirement will return to their country of birth, there to spend their retirement pay? As a public policy issue this fiscal flow is limited to social security and other government programs. But as a fiscal issue it applies to private retirement pay as well.

An American by birth on retirement receives Social Security and Medicare benefits and continues to buy goods and services mostly made by American workers and to pay income, property, sales and excise taxes. If he were to move to warmer climes in some Caribbean nation, he would still receive social security, but would pay no U.S. taxes. Most of his spending would employ workers in his retirement country. He would not receive Medicare benefits, but the lower medical costs in his new place of residence could more than make up for lost benefits. No big problem, not many emigrants.

Consider instead the many millions of immigrants from Latin America. Economic immigrants are mainly young adults. Suppose quite a few millions, after working here for many years, chose to retire in their country of origin. The loss of tax revenue might be a problem for some jurisdictions. The decline in consumer spending would reduce the number of jobs. Should eligibility for social security payments be linked to country of residence? Of course not, it is a contributory right. But the economic consequences should be kept in mind. There are many reasons for emigration on retirement, but difference in cost of living is number one.

Countries of emigration face both fiscal and demographic problems. Fiscally much depends on domestic alternatives for prospective emigrants - would they be working, paying taxes, or unemployed? If they migrate, no longer paying taxes or burdening government services, how large will be their remittances? Large enough to compensate for loss of consumption and tax revenues had they stayed? What proportion return in later years bringing retirement income from the country in which they worked?

POPULATION FLOWS AND DEPENDENCY RATIOS

Emigration reduces the labor force in the country of emigration, increases it in the country of immigration. It may affect fertility. As to retirement migration, the destination gains, the origin of retirees loses. Is either worker or retiree migration flow a problem big enough to require policy choices? Much depends on fertility rates.

Emigration of working age persons from Latin America to the United States was not a problem in the past. Many were unemployed at home, and fertility was so high and longevity low that the dependency ratio (population over 65 and under 15 divided by population 15-65) was low. But now fertility rates for the largest countries are at or below replacement level. Only a few nations with small populations have fertility rates much above replacement. Extensive emigration will raise dependency rates beyond desirable levels. Immigrant remittances, which are temporary, may not be adequate compensation. There is a similar decline of fertility in Muslim countries. Among large countries only Pakistan has a fertility rate well above replacement, and Egypt somewhat above.

Voluntary decline in fertility almost worldwide, below replacement levels in much of the world, has no historical precedent. We do not know how future generations will behave. Migration, which once redistributed population growth, is beginning to redistribute population totals. Many nations will be declining in population, seeking immigrants; others will become reluctant to see any of their people leave. The supply of would be immigrants still vastly exceeds demand, but the disparity is diminishing. This nation has never limited the right to emigrate. Given its history it is unthinkable that it should. But other nations do, for political reasons today, for economic reasons in the future. Once Japan, then other nations, reach a point where population 65 and older is one third of the population, either it must find a way to drastically reduce the costs of sustaining unproductive elders or so burden the declining number of taxpayers that they acquire a strong incentive to emigrate.

A rising dependency ratio is good, since the world is overpopulated in terms of a decent standard of living for all. It quadrupled in the last century and low fertility is the best way to bring this growth to a halt. But the adjustment process entails slower growth or actual decline in living levels. In the next few decades, fear of shrinkage has an economic rationale. In the longer run, different nations and population groups will resist declining relative to others. They will invent fertility rights and obligations, reconsider abortion rights. As more nations compete for a shrinking pool of migrants we can anticipate debates over national identity, demographic disputes, perhaps population wars between countries whose borders have changed in the past century.

Most nations were originally tribal, and most still are tribal, or multi-tribal. This may still be true of Europe. The Gypsies have been living in almost every European nation for many centuries, but nowhere have they been integrated in the larger society. An implication for the decades ahead is that immigrants are not a simple solution for low fertility and declining labor force if a society is unwilling or unable to assimilate them.

Chapter 24

WHO AM I?

What is the identity of a nation's citizens? Nearly all nations were originally tribes, their identity ethnic- historical. The United States is unique: not tribal, still in the process of becoming historical. Its identity is ideological, embodied in the Declaration of Independence and the Constitution. But this identity is shared with millions, it is not personal. Within a country, how do people characterize themselves?

The United States is individualistic; nations of tribal roots are more communal. But individualism can be tempered by concern for the neighborhood or larger community, as in the United States, or it can be undiluted egocentricity, in nations I shall not name. Community itself can be a hierarchical concept; a sense of community may mean nuclear family (China), extended family, clan, or extend to the neighborhood, to the entire nation (Japan).

Cultural differences matter for behavior in two ways. They influence the nature and magnitude of the problems a society must face, and they influence what policies are feasible. For instance, some democratic nations are much more willing to pay taxes than others; to work long hours, years. They differ in tolerance of high unemployment, of declines in income, of inequality, in the willingness of labor to organize, in the size and role of government, in acceptance of "paternalism" or government initiative and responsibility. What works in one country may not work in another.

Look at Northern vs. Southern Europe today. Problems considered trivial in one are regarded as traumatic in another; policies that work in one fail in another or simply are not adopted. What we can learn from the experience of others must be filtered through the lens of culture.

FAMILY NAMES

We can learn something about these cultural differences by looking at choices of family names as an indication of the culture at the time they were created. There is little question that a culture can persist indefinitely in its original habitat. How do individuals identify themselves, what is their sense of identity? How do they differentiate themselves from others with the same first name? But the relation between names, culture, and policy agenda is more a research proposal than a finding.

A second name may have been a means of asserting individuality, distinguishing oneself from others with the same "first" name. Tom the bald, or the baker, or the Samaritan selected by others was not initially a family name, but an identifier of the individual, who shared first name with others.

Personal identity became a social issue with urbanization. Too many people had the same "first" name. In a face to face community, second names were unnecessary. But as communities grew too large for face to face interaction, and as interactions grew with other communities, it became necessary to develop a formal system of identification. Second names became a public issue at the time when governments required that its citizens have a second name. How could the tax collector know who had paid taxes, who had not? Many other government functions required individual identification: birth and death certification, voter registration, the draft. As more children were born it became a matter of convenience for family, community, and government to convert the second name of the father into the family name.

The choice of classification was influenced by the structure and culture of society at the time. A geographic/nature classification would be appropriate for rural populations: few occupations, many areas, and local features. An occupational classification would be more appropriate for urban areas: numerous individuals in the same area, but diverse occupations. The order of personal name and family name tells us much about the society. We designate personal name as first name, family name as last name. It is the sequence characteristic of an individualistic society. East Asian family name comes first, personal names last. This suggests a family identification stronger than any in Europe.

Casually, family names cluster in 3 categories: occupational, as in England and Germany; family (descended from), as in southern Europe, and locational names. (A few, such as Smithson, relate to the ancestor's occupation rather than proper name.) Occupational names, as in England and Germany, imply an individualistic culture and self-identification via occupation.

Occupation is about the present. "Descended from" names, found in most southern European countries, is about the past.

Family names based on location: town, region, or local features - vegetation, topography, such as Hill, Field, do not distinguish between the individual and the group. They have an element of stasis, passivity vs. effort, activity. Big places as family names lack exclusivity, specificity. Was Jack London, Irving Berlin their real names? Sgt. York, yes. Not sure they are widespread anywhere. There are too many Smiths and Joneses today, too many Johnsons and Harrisons. So we are all issued a social security number at birth.

What family names today can tell us about culture and conditions at their time of selection is whether all the occupations are represented, whether the names of towns and regions at the time are fully represented, and whether all male first personal names in use at the time became family names. The demographic history of particular family names varies widely. Today's distribution of family names may not reflect its original distribution. But it is highly unlikely that those with occupational names and those with "descended from" names or locational names would have significantly different population growth rates in a given nation. Their distribution in a nation gives a sense of national identity, be it economic, geographical, or historical/genetic.

Immigrants

Nations of immigrants are different. Their family names are imported and provide little clue to individual or national sense of identity. The early immigrants to this country came from northern Europe, and Africa. Later immigration was from central and southern Europe. More recently, immigrants flooded from Central America, followed by new arrivals from Asia.

Culture in its native habitat may persist indefinitely, but after an ocean crossing it becomes malleable, measured in generations. It must come to terms with other cultures, conditions. Family names can still inform us about differences between communities of different ethnic composition. Hispanic communities are more family-oriented than others, as their names would suggest. Anglo-German communities are more occupation-oriented. This very diversity makes it more difficult to design policies and programs that are widely accepted and highly effective. If arriving at consensus on cost-sharing is so difficult at home, it becomes impossible internationally, as in the case of climate policy and many other issues. Nations of immigrants may lack the cultural coherence of their countries of origin, which facilitate consensus on policies and goals. They are individualistic, but also future-oriented, willing to take risks, share a passion for novelty, a demand for innovation. Private policies, that do not require consensus, can be more important in their history than in the nations of tribal origin. Multi-tribal nations share with nations of immigrants the great difficulty of consensus, even more so since their separate ethnicities remain rooted in their native soil. But they are likely to lack the future orientation, the passion for change.

FUTURE

The sources of personal identity are in the minds of individuals, not in their names. Past sources of identity are devalued today. Take place names. The population was almost entirely rural when family names were first chosen. Most lived out their lives close to their place of birth. Then came urbanization which depopulated the countryside, and industrialization, which moved jobs and workers from place to place. Where are you from? is a common greeting, indicating that everyone is expected to have come from somewhere else.

Occupations are no longer inherited; the distribution of workers by occupation has changed dramatically. Not many Smiths hammer on an anvil, few Farmers ever plowed an acre. When names were chosen, most individuals worked all their live\s at the same occupation. Now old occupations disappear, new ones multiply, many yet to find a name or recognition in the public eye. "What do you do? Not "What is your occupation or trade?"

In the past workers labored until they died or as long as they were physically able. Now workers may spend a year in retirement for every two years of labor. During their working years they have weekends off, and vacations. Their working days are no longer 10 or 12 hours, They have much time on their hands. This time and the uses to which the individual puts it provide a source of identity alternative to family, place, occupation.

Families have fewer descendants, will have fewer ancestors. A family name is typically that of the father. There is always a mother. With the liberation of women, the mother's family name is important too. Proliferation of single parents also promotes the mother's family name.

Formerly, marriages were predominantly among those who lived near each other, who shared ethnic, social, cultural backgrounds. Now married couples are much more diversified. Progeny have a variety of family backgrounds with which they are entitled to identify; they have a choice of culture, ethnicity, and perhaps of name. Family identity is not given at birth. Women in particular are no longer home-bound and thus occupational identity becomes an option. The growth of single child families, single parent households, reduction in the number of close relatives downgrades the role of family in the life of many individuals.

What does it matter? First, the uses to which one puts one's leisure have a major impact on consumption, therefore on what is produced, what jobs are available. Second, leisure time uses shape social networks and foster the creation and growth of support organizations.

Ancestry is not the individual's choice. Neither is place of birth and childhood. Jobs and occupations may not be chosen. They are likely to change over a working life, but the individual does not change identity. Thus it makes sense in this nation to identify with the choices one makes of the uses of a significant part of one's life. If current trends persist, the retired may eventually constitute one third of voting age population. Their culture will matter for national policy.

Occupation, generation, habitation remain primary identifying traits of most individuals. But it is rather pathetic for individuals twenty years retired still identifying themselves, or being characterized by others, in terms of occupation. For those who move on retirement, what is location? Birth, work, retirement home? Only in leisure time and in retirement can we be what we like.

Chapter 25

SOLITUDE

The paper has not been picked up all week. Perhaps I should call, or ring the bell. But suppose there is no paper, just a mail slot. Utility bills pile up inside, unpaid. Or the resident has bills paid by his bank from the retirement pay and social security checks deposited in his account. Months may pass unnoticed. Perhaps a dog keeps barking, but cats don't bark. Someone is very sick, or dead inside, no one knows or cares. This tragedy happens sometimes in this country, and in Europe. It could become quite frequent. It could be you or me.

People move. They do not know their neighbors. People live alone in much larger numbers than before. One of every five households has a single person. Throughout the advanced world a rising share of adults have no children. They may have no one with whom to live, no one who keeps tabs on their existence. Three generation families are prehistoric; two generation adults in a single household an endangered species. Individualism run amuck.

We have institutions for the sick, institutions for the senile, for those who can afford them. Collectivism is substituting for community, nurse's aides for family. If the burden of the elderly rises high, who can afford the time and cost of progeny? It is a self-reinforcing spiral of isolation.

We are one-dimensional creatures. We know our fellow workers. But should they leave, or should I change jobs, all trace of their existence is erased from my hippocampus. I know the parents of my children's school and playmates, until they move or graduate. My Rolodex is full of names of persons whose existence I have forgotten. Once they played some role in my life, it is my own life I have forgotten.

Must I live forever in the transient present? One-dimensional experiences become one-dimensional memories, working memories, they are short, no wonder they don't imprint, leave no trace.

Our fertility is just below replacement rate. All we need change is the practice of association. Traditional association was generational and consanguineous. But now many seniors have no children, many juniors have no sibling, and their number is expected to grow. Numbers apart, the practice of multi-generational households has declined. With the weakening bonds of blood, could Facebook be part of the answer, or are electronic associations of strangers a reflection of the problem of isolation, not a solution? Neighborhood awareness, neighborhood organization is the way to go; place of residence, not e-mail address. Ideally there would be no need, individuals would adapt their behavior to strengthen networks of common activities, common interests. But neighborhood oversight would be a fallback option. Let no one go unnoticed, be alone. Do we want to follow the example of the Japanese, whose fertility is much lower than ours, and open a business "Relatives for Rent" or follow Milton Friedman's advice, " buy a friend"?

There are nations in Asia whose fertility rate is little more than half replacement rates. Fortunately they have a much stronger sense and practice of community than we do. But with each new generation considerably smaller than its predecessor, the breakdown of association, community, becomes unbearable. There must be more children, or more immigrants. But they are overpopulated, and fewer children is the only socially and ethically acceptable means of reducing numbers. In China, single children grow up less altruistic, less trusting, enterprising, optimistic than their predecessors with siblings and more relatives. The dilemma of this century is the conflict between means to a necessary goal and its unintended consequences.

For individual longevity we can think of no civilized solution. The terminal solitude of those whose bodies live on but whose minds have fled is no burden for the living dead but for those they left behind.

Chapter 26

ON LIVING TOO LONG

The demographic future is not just about fertility, it also reflects changes in longevity. The ballooning costs of medical care are driving down the resources available for all other purposes, both private and public. A discussion of misuses and abuses of medical care needs to be book-length. Here I address just one major issue: dysfunctional longevity.

This problem is older than the human species, but in the past it was on a small scale, and a family problem. Now the scale is large, bound to grow much larger, and a social problem, beyond the capabilities of most families. As an unintended byproduct of public health and medical care, many more people become dysfunctional but live on. There are two terminal states short of the grave:

1. The mind is still lit, but the body is unresponsive to its orders.
2. The mind has fled the brain but the body persists on automatic reflexes.

These are the easy cases. Most cases are intermediate. A mind that flickers but no longer flames, that sleeps but might conceivably awaken; a body still responsive to the brain but some of whose functions are impaired "sans eyes, sans teeth, sans everything"

Terminal state #1 should be up to the individual concerned, who is capable of making decisions. Such an individual should have a practical and legal choice, to live or die. Society must learn to regard this freedom of choice as moral. The responsibility is the individual's, whoever executes the individual's choice. Terminal state #2: the individual is gone, the body is mindless. The burden of decision cannot be placed exclusively on the family.

How define family? Sometimes there is no close relative in any case. Then it is a public responsibility, which may be delegated to relatives or health services providers.

Who should pay? In the first case, the individual should pay if he/she chooses to live, until assets are exhausted, at which point Medicaid takes over. Whatever changes may be made in health care in the future, it is inconceivable that the society should allow such an individual to starve or freeze to death. But who can afford it?

The cost of nursing homes can be two to three times the median earnings of a full time full year worker. This means that in the vast majority of cases, payment must be through depletion of savings, sale of assets, or accumulation of debt. Only a tiny minority of the population, on the order of three or four percent, would be able to pay for prolonged nursing care out of current income, and even most of these would have to adjust their living styles. For the rest, their wills are no more than expressions of hope, their estates only a probability.

The fact that the average number of children has declined to just under two, and many seniors have no children, reduces the possibilities of family financing of nursing home, or provision of family home care.

In the second case, the state assumes the responsibility; there may be no alternative, no immediate family, or relatives may be unable to pay. It must have the legal authority to terminate treatment and life if it can make a case that the status is irreversible. Any family would retain the right to assume responsibility for maintaining life support.

This may sound like a cost/benefit approach to life. It may well be, from the point of the individual and family, as long as they are paying, experiencing depletion of income and assets, foreseeing evaporation of estates. But once the patient is on Medicaid, patient and family concern is only about benefit – the quality of life – which may be negative as well as positive. The payer – the state – is concerned with cost and cost alone. A cost-benefit calculation requires a common currency, and neither dollars nor quality of life can fit the bill.

The generation now in nursing homes, born between the two world wars, is small. Its successor, the baby boom generation, is almost twice as large. It is also longer lived, has fewer children, and did not inherit the habit of saving. What is possible for the former, financing of nursing care by Medicaid, may not be possible for the latter. The decline of marriage – increased number of single person households, and single parent households – further shifts the burden from the household to the state, which already faces chronic deficits.

There is no benefit in prolonging the life of the body when the mind is gone. Senility is a curse. Geriatric research should concentrate on the mind.

Advanced nations are dealing effectively with one unintended consequence of public health and medical care: population growth. Their fertility rates are at or below replacement level. They have yet to face the other unintended consequence: dysfunctional longevity. The solution of the first problem increases the burden of the second by increasing the dependency ratio. Transfer of resources from factories, farms and offices to nursing homes is the final battle in a war between generations.

The demands of the elderly should not deprive the young of opportunity or ability to succeed in a competitive world. Such demands would be self-defeating. The right to die lessens the conflict between young and old. Today there are too many rights, but this is one we lack.

Individuals must be granted the ultimate freedom, of ending their own lives when they are no longer worth living, a burden on themselves as well as others. Society, via changes in attitude and law, must come to terms with dysfunctional longevity. Other societies have done so often in rather brutal ways; we can learn to celebrate a long life well ended instead of the misery of years in a nursing home.

Chapter 27

IN DEFENSE OF MARRIAGE

What is the cost of survival past retirement age? For most seniors much of the time it is simple: the cost of living. But for some, and for most toward the end of their lives, it is much more. They are physically or mentally incompetent, or both, and require care to compensate for loss of mobility, or for decline in memory, and for other physical and cognitive deficiencies. Such care is in addition to medical costs of the illnesses common among the elderly.

The cost of senescence should nearly triple for the next generation, absent some magical breakthrough in staving off dementia. The same is true of the cost of physical debility. The baby boom generation is almost twice as large as its predecessor as the depression-WWII generation and longer-lived.

The responsibility and burden initially falls on the immediate family. But the baby boom generation has fewer children and other close relatives on whom to rely in old age that its predecessors. The state is recourse of last resort, as the representative of society.

There is a missing variable: marriage. The large increase in proportion of single person households, and single parent families, shifts all these responsibilities toward the public sector. Medicaid will start ballooning next year anyway. Nursing home for advanced cases can be $12,000 a month, three times the median earnings of full time full year workers. To assume that Medicaid can pay much longer is burying your head in the sand.

What to do? Everyone should be married. Same-sex marriage is a step in this direction. Whatever one's view on homosexuality and legal marriage of homosexuals, it is better to live together than to live alone. No one should be alone, responsible for no one else and in turn having no one to fall back on. Some status in addition to traditional monogamy is needed to deal with the fact that sex ratios vary by community and by any criterion of eligibility (education, age, race, religion, etc.)

There is also a shortage of men who are willing to assume the responsibilities of paternity. A tax on bachelors? No, regressive. I suggest considering legalization of bigamy (and biandry). It is widely practiced as it is. (Polygamy is a stretch too far.) Then the legal, economic, and moral responsibility for care of the physically and/or mentally incompetent would shift toward the private sector. This requires a major change in attitudes. Many cultures, especially in Africa, have practices to assure that no woman is alone; the core of Mormon polygamy was that all women should be and remain married. Such a practice could apply to men as well in the 21st century of demographic decline.

Some couples marrying late have already accumulated substantial assets. They arrange for a special quasi-marriage legal status that gives them the advantages of marriage but preserves their assets from depletion in behalf of the other partner. No joint property. Yes, it reduces the legal and economic shift toward the private sector, but the private moral responsibility remains intact.

What about the unmarried mothers? Some states impose legal responsibility for the child on the father. Better if it were a national policy. A legal offensive is needed to insure that men who father children share responsibility for their upbringing. Such a requirement would reduce the number of unintended and unwanted births. DNA can determine paternity if there is doubt or dispute. Obtaining the necessary sample from the alleged father is a legal issue. The father cannot be required to marry (there may be more than one father) but should be required to contribute to support.

Whether by marriage or other means, let there be an end to solitary confinement.

Humans are social animals. No human should be alone. Every human being should have at least one other on whom to rely in case of need; every competent adult should be responsible for the wellbeing of at least another human being. This is not community, but individualism tempered by mutual concern. We do not want a nation of narcissists ending their lives on Medicaid in nursing homes. Mutual responsibility is the basic building block of a functioning society and of all morality.

Chapter 28

RESTRUCTURING SOCIETY

The fundamental challenge of the century is the growth of public sector commitments for pensions and elderly health care made impossible by the decline in fertility plus increase in longevity. The issue of inequality, once about work incomes, is now primarily one between workers and non-workers. It cannot be addressed in terms of the Gini coefficient. The income of the elderly may be no higher than that of the working population, probably will be lower. But it will be sustained by transfer of worker income via taxation. The elderly will also be receiving health and other services most of whose costs will be paid by others, namely taxpayers. This transfer has negative consequences for investment and work incentives. Work incentives may be further weakened by government subsidies for higher education, unemployment compensation for the unemployed, Food Stamps and other subsidies for low income households. We should consider how these objectives might be pursued with minimal unwanted and unintended consequences.

The choice is between diminution of entitlements and default. Inflation or prolonged default is how we have paid for wars. But wars end. Promises for pensions, health care, subsidies for higher education continue indefinitely. Inflation simply increases their money costs. It is the promises that must be devalued, not the currency.

What should be done?

First, shift functions and services from the public sector to the family and household economy as much as possible.

Second, shift resources and functions from the public sector to the private market and non-market sector as much as possible.

Third, having reduced somewhat the burden of entitlements, reform government organization and decision making in the image of the private firm; consider both costs and benefits, long run as well as short run.

Fourth, if still necessary, cut or limit the entitlements themselves to society's ability and willingness to pay for them.

HOUSEHOLDS

The decline in fertility means a decline in the average size of households. The resulting decline in population is desirable on a long term basis from a global standpoint, to reduce depletion of resources and human impact on climate.

Population growth is not a desirable solution. There has been a large increase in single-person and single-generation households, a large increase in single-parent households as well. The implication is that households are much less able to cope with illness or long term debility of a family member; needed help is outsourced to hospitals, nursing homes, and assisted living facilities. The household economy has lost economies of scale and scope.

No one should be alone. We should encourage two and three generation households. In a geographically mobile economy the prospects of three-generation households are limited. We should consider other means to provide non-market support for the ill, the disabled, the unemployed. There is a growing supply of retirees in good health with spare time who could be engaged in useful volunteer activities. Local community action should supplement or substitute for family and household help. Community associations or religious groups or local governments should organize a voluntary work force and contributions to meet local needs. This is a very local, retail enterprise.

Empowerment of the household, family and local voluntary community could significantly reduce the costs of entitlements to governments and taxpayers.

The detached family house hampers community by reducing proximity and is also wasteful of energy in itself and via required car mileage. Dispersed residence should be discouraged especially in cities with declining population.

The increase in longevity has also created a moral problem for society. Too many will spend years physically and/or mentally dysfunctional. This is a growing burden that offers no countervailing benefit, just prolonged misery. Find means to reduce the problem, not just to deal with it. Nations with low fertility whose workers are prone to emigrate will have no choice. In an individualist society, an elderly or dysfunctional individual or his guardian should be free to end a life categorically not worth living. Communitarian societies need a counterpart procedure.

ENTITLEMENTS

The model of an organization in a free society that is able to plan long run to avoid such dilemmas, and to resolve them should they arise, is the private competitive enterprise. It is democratic; it responds to a continuing referendum on performance, namely sales and other indicators of the behavior and attitudes of its customers. Its decision making and the selection of decision makers is influenced by its owners, whose votes are weighted by their share holdings. Investment capital may be profits of the enterprise, borrowed money, or sale of additional shares. The last method, sometimes referred to as stock watering, is analogous to inflation as a means of reducing the burden of debt by printing money.

But the private analogy to a pension entitlement is not the company struggling to survive in an economic jungle full of fierce competitors, subject to technological evolution, product change, shifting demands. Instead, it is the staid public utility that can charge rates covering its costs, with assured profits limited by regulators, not subject to a political process. Such an enterprise plans long term but is capable of adjusting promptly to changes in circumstances. It has the incentives to do so, and the resources. Adaptability is essential because long term plans are about probabilities, not certainties.

The main loss-loss situation facing governments in most other nations is retirement pensions. For us it is not just Social Security but state government pensions. It was precisely predictable and perfectly avoidable. We have increased the payroll tax as far as we dare go, and taken a small step toward a higher retirement age. This deficit is easily soluble by some combination of higher retirement age, taxation of benefits, progressivity of benefits, and a higher ceiling, or no ceiling, on salaries subject to payroll tax. But the political will is lacking. It fits the public utility model.

Millions receiving pensions in the early 22nd century are in kindergarten right now. Thus long term pension cost projections are possible, later adjusted for small changes in longevity and net immigration. A single institution should be authorized to make all necessary adjustments in revenues and benefits, subject to periodic review and reauthorization.

In our case, but not in Europe, the biggest loss-loss challenge is Medicare. The aging of the population was predictable. Most of the ballooning of health care costs was not, but it was hardly a surprise, since it has been ballooning for forty years. The health care industry is highly inefficient and, some would say, corrupt. We spend far more than any other country. Its costs must be brought under control if there is any hope of perpetuating the Medicare (and Medicaid) entitlement.

The first and most important step is to make the prices for every pill and procedure charged by every provider known to every patient and payer. The second is to create an incentive to economize on costs, not just prices but in procedures and medication. HMOs have such incentives. Patients with Medicare lack the information and, if they have secondary insurance, lack the incentives.

Medicare (and Medicaid) is only the fiscal part of the problem. The economic problem is health care costs driving down disposable income of the working population. Competition is essential, and information a requirement. Most of the cost inflation is attributable to "nonprofit" organizations, hospitals especially. Since colleges driving up tuition costs are also nonprofit, perhaps the rationale for nonprofit status should be reconsidered.

In Europe, health care systems are dominated by public health care. It is removed from the political process. But in the United States, health care supply is predominantly in private hands whereas much of the demand for health care is financed by governments. There is a difference in culture that precludes adoption of a British-type National Health Service. The public utility model does not fit; too many products, processes, providers.

In this nation, insurance premiums are not related to income; elsewhere, financing is via taxation, which is progressive. But Medicaid is an alternative approach for the poor. Health care is our second largest industry; it is catching up with the largest, which is government.

What, beyond Medicaid (and welfare, unemployment compensation) is to be done do about inequality? This is an ethical or ideological issue. How much inequality should there be? Cutting health costs would reduce inequality of disposable income, inasmuch as the share of income spent on health care is inversely related to income. Millions pay more in health insurance than in federal income taxes. The federal income tax itself is far less progressive than it seems. But the initial earnings distribution is not the government's business. Its influence is indirect; education and training is the principal vehicle.

The state is the ultimate recourse. But why should individuals abandon personal responsibility, delegate authority and responsibility to the state? At one time citizen rights were few and general: life, liberty and pursuit. Is there liberty without responsibility? Individuals, not just governments, should plan long term and respond promptly to changing circumstances. A citizen who out-sources responsibility and authority is self-deprived of autonomy. Is this what we mean by democracy?

If governments do not act on the basis of the long term, perhaps it is because citizens think only short term, demand rights, and assume no responsibility. Have governments created a new kind of irresponsible citizenry, or is it the citizens who have created this sort of government? A government of rights is in conflict with reality.

Chapter 29

CHINESE CHECKERS

Not in living memory has any nation faced so many serious long term problems than today's China. These problems cannot be ignored or postponed. What makes them supremely difficult to face is the fact that they interact and conflict with one another.

Consider first the environment. The air in large cities and industrial areas is so polluted – a large multiple of acceptable limits at times – that health is harmed, life expectancy in the industrial northeast reduced by five years, and no doubt infant mortality is increased. It is not just the air, or urban areas. The overuse of chemicals in agricultural areas, apart from polluting the water supply and the soil itself, have killed so many bugs and birds that in some areas tree crops are reported to have been pollinated by hand. This situation raises questions whether the resulting fruit is fit to eat or a slow poison. The main conflict is with production: less pesticides, fewer smokestacks mean less output, possibly fewer jobs.

A second major problem is the acute shortage of women of marriageable age, which cannot be changed for a generation or more. Although blamed on the one-child policy, it has deep cultural roots particularly in agriculture, which persist in urban life. Without changing this attitude, it will continue as long as parents can determine the sex of a fetus and obtain abortions. This shortage promotes a kidnapping industry, young women, some married, shipped to a distant location and sold as brides. It also increases rape. But far more dangerous is the persistence of many millions of young men who have no chance of marriage, and are social and political tinder.

Overcoming the bias in favor of sons is probably impossible with the one-child policy. If possible at all, it would increase fertility and promote population growth in a nation already greatly overpopulated. The shortage of marriageable women is aggravated by Chinese preference for very young brides and women's increased educational and occupational attainment.

Another problem promoting unrest among the young, males in particular, is the huge increase in the numbers of college graduates, with a large and possibly increasing proportion unable to obtain jobs or occupations commensurate with their education or expectations. An educated partly unemployed and unemployable underclass is even more dangerous to social stability than young men without women. But placing limits on college admissions in keeping with projected employment prospects could be a hugely unpopular policy.

The low fertility rate means that each generation is smaller than its predecessor, in time resulting in a declining labor force and an increase in the dependency ratio: the population not of working age divided by the working age population. There are pressures to relax the one-child policy, but plans to move 250 million rural residents to urban areas will reduce fertility. The very low rates in Hong Kong, Taiwan, South Korea, Japan, lower than China's, although they have no policy, suggest that even abandoning the policy may not raise fertility to replacement rate. Low fertility is not just a policy outcome. It accompanies industrialization, urbanization, and increased educational achievement.

The conflict between problems and solutions is nowhere more acute than in demography. Low fertility is a partial solution to the environmental pollution problem, a requirement to bring population numbers down, but it means a decline in growth of per capita income and might even reduce per capita income in some future years.

The decline in the labor force resulting from low fertility tends to raise wages; higher labor costs in turn reduce the ability to compete in world export markets. At this time, Chinese economic growth requires not only a very high level of exports, but an increasing level. High labor costs militate against both. Meanwhile other nations with cheap labor are improving their ability to compete against China for exports, and also for imports. The result is upward pressure on the cost of imports, downward pressure on the price of exports. This is a process that cannot be reversed or stopped, at best it can be slowed down. Adjustment must take the form of restructuring the Chinese economy to depend less on exports and imports, more on domestic consumption. But a consumption-driven economy involves a major shift of power from the public to the market sector. The victim is authoritarianism and Communist party control. Finally, China is at a disadvantage in a future of global communication and information, as long as it relies on a cumbersome writing system ill-suited for the use of computer technology.

What should be done? Concentrate on the problems subject to abatement if not resolution. This means environmental improvement, a shift of the economy from overinvestment to consumer goods and services for domestic consumption, and educational reform, providing skills for the economy but avoiding oversupply of graduates. The first two pose no political problems, but limiting over-education would not be popular. Decline in growth of exports is only a problem if the economy does not shift toward compensating domestic consumption.

The demographic problem: low fertility, rising dependency ratio, is long run, and probably beyond government control.

Chinese history is not encouraging; it reveals a persistent inability to change, reluctance to adapt. Contrast it with Japan. Japan for centuries was a closed society – closed to foreigners, foreign technology. Samurai master swordsmen were no match for peasants bearing guns, so guns were banned. But when Perry's black warships steamed into Edo, the Japanese made a 180 degree turn, sending emissaries abroad to master modern technology, rapidly industrializing and becoming an imperial power. China by contrast suffered humiliation at the hands of European nations for centuries: loss of territory, trade control, but lumbered on, kow-towing to new masters as it did to the old. The guiding principle of Chinese rule is stability, and stability conflicts with change. But major change is coming, imposed from outside if not also initiated at home.

A major concern is that China will follow the practice of authoritarian governments elsewhere when threatened or faced with internal unrest. They provoke foreign disputes, even initiate wars, to divert domestic attention from internal problems. Chinese concepts of national rights have little respect for human rights.

Chapter 30

The War of Words

The destiny of species is extinction. Should biologists reconstruct the saber-toothed tiger by manipulating the genes of existing felines, where would it roam and hunt, what species would it devour to extinction? Humans are great creators of species. Some of them are called inventions, which rapidly replace one another, from stick to spear to bow to firearm. Their most important invention is language, of which there are many, in a final struggle for survival and supremacy. Linguists besiege the last speakers of a dying tongue, to record it. What for - will it ever be spoken again?

To survive in the 21st century, a language must be written and read. How much will be written, never mind printed, for a potential readership of a few thousands? There are great economies of scale in the competition between languages and the minimal viable scale keeps rising with the multiplication of human knowledge. Gutenberg initiated the age of mega-languages. Efforts to create new international languages, such as Esperanto, no one's native language, are bound to fail because there is very little to read, and very few for whom to write.

The languages of primitive peoples lack the cognitive, information resources to express and disseminate modern knowledge. In their case, competitive extinction is survival of the fit. But other languages are victims of the economic backwardness of their society or its conquest by other peoples, or demographic decline. Bigger is better.

In the Western Hemisphere, once home to thousands of languages, there are 3: English, Spanish and Portuguese, plus French enclaves dependent on readers elsewhere. Several Indian languages – Maya, Quechua, Aymara, Guarani - are still spoken by quite a few million people. But the press in their countries is predominantly in Spanish, without which there is little access to world knowledge.

In Africa, there are four languages: English, French, Portuguese and Arabic. Hundreds of local languages are spoken still, but the newspapers and books are in these four, primarily English and French except for North Africa. If there is any African language with some survival value it is Amharic, but its potential scope is limited to Ethiopia.

In Europe most nations have a large enough reading public to support newspapers and magazines in their own language, even should only the larger countries: Germany, Russia, Italy, in addition to the Western Hemisphere languages, have an ample range of other published material in their own language. Most educated Europeans can read in more than one language. There is a pressing need for a common language shared by Europeans, this need is being met by English, and there is no prospect that it will be replaced by another language this century. The difference in survival prospects of European languages spoken by few people and the Amerindian languages is that the Europeans became literate centuries ago and established a printed literature in their own language. In the Western hemisphere, literacy lagged, and was almost always in European languages.

In Asia, the scripts of China and Japan preclude linguistic adoption elsewhere. The cost of learning and maintaining fluency in their logograms is just too high. China's cultural and aesthetic attachment to its ancient script is strong; its monosyllabic vocabulary has many homonyms. It is large enough to translate all the world's knowledge into its own script. But for China to have any linguistic influence commensurate with its economic or political power, it must adopt a phonetic script. Japan has adopted English as its doorway to the rest of the world. India is a nation of many languages. Publication for a mass readership can persist in several Indian languages, in their own script, but English is well established as the lingua franca. As to other populous nations in Asia, each has its own language or languages, not shared with other nations. None have full access to world knowledge in their own tongue. Pakistan, Bangladesh, Malaysia rely on English. Indonesia, the world's fourth most populous nation, does not seem likely to translate most of the world's literature into Bahasa Indonesia, the national language of a polyglot archipelago.

English is the imperialist language of our time, for political, economic, and technological reasons. The other imperialist European language, Russian, and its Cyrillic script, is in retreat. Only time will tell whether the mastery of the language imposed by the Russian, then Soviet, empire will persist in the five Central Asian nations, in the Trans-Caucasian nations. It appears doomed in Eastern Europe.

The dominance of English as the world language is self-reinforcing. Anyone seeking international readership is under pressure to write and publish in English, which will become the one language in which all world knowledge is available. The Roman script has already become the world script. The only phonetic alternative, Arabic, was doomed by the decadence of Arabic-speaking nations. Most languages now spoken will disappear by the end of the century or be spoken only by the elderly.

Those languages spoken by enough people to support a daily newspaper and similar mass market publications, to support widely viewed programming on internet, radio, TV, will linger a little longer., But educated speakers will also have a reading knowledge of a global language. Apart from these publications and the transactions of government little else will be written for publication. Novelists, poets, scholarly authors who may speak the language at home will write in a global tongue if they wish to be read. If nearly all writing and most reading is done in a global language, it is inevitable that speech will follow.

In the world of mathematics there is already one world language. The same is true of the shared notations in separate fields of science. In the past, languages have evolved and subdivided. Evolve they will, but instant mass communications should preclude their fissiparous proclivities.

Chapter 31

WARS IN THE 21ST CENTURY

For half a century the United States was the policeman for much of the world. No one knows how many wars were prevented. Some were cut short. But now that the policeman has retired expect a proliferation of robberies and murders. We are beginning to see this. I suspect it began in the late 1990s when the policeman went on vacation. The US decided to let North Korea go ahead with the nuclear bomb after it flagrantly violated the agreement it had signed in 1994. It now has an ICBM and we are firing back UN resolutions. Ouch.

The policeman role requires three things: the capability, the will, and the credibility. Without credibility there is no prevention, there may be punishment. By now, credibility has been lost. Unfortunately there is no way of restoring credibility other than military. I don't think there is any other way to stop Iran or any other nation from developing and deploying nuclear weapons.

At present there is no will. Without the will, credibility cannot be restored or maintained. The 21st century will see much warfare. Yet much progress was made in the twentieth century. War in the Western Hemisphere seems unthinkable. The wars of the dissolution of Yugoslavia in the 1990s may be the last European wars. That is up to Russia.

What wars should we anticipate? First, and most dangerous, is Chinese expansion and conquest, resource wars. Second, the wars we see beginning today, Islamic wars of rejection of the values and institutions of western civilization, longing for return to the past, a past which never existed. Third, the Malthusian wars of overpopulation, mainly in Africa, as disease and starvation fail to slow growth. There is little we can do unless they spill over, as does piracy off Somalia.

CHINA

The age of imperialism is over. The two main imperial nations remaining are China and Indonesia, or the Javanese empire. Java once lusted for Borneo and for Papua New Guinea, and perhaps some still do, but it would not be a major threat to world peace. Some Russians may dream of extending their rule to former Soviet republics, but that is nostalgia, a dream, not a policy. Another chunk of Georgia, perhaps the Crimea, eastern Ukraine would be as far as the current regime would dare go. China on the other hand claims most of the South China Sea, even claims rights to artic resources; it has attacked several of its neighbors in the past 60 years, is hostile to several, and is preparing for war with the United States. It is surrounded by numerous nations all of which fear it, and most of which hate it. Not a nice picture, but the current regime does not seem to care about popularity.

It is very dependent on import of resources, including feed and food, for continued growth, and must export in order to pay for its imports. It is the Japan of the 21st Century. As it grows, imports will become more costly and export earnings more difficult to maintain. The trade option was once rejected by Japan. The other option is to follow the Japanese path of conquest. Five thousand years of authoritarian tradition bias Chinese thinking toward control rather than trade. The European empires in Asia no longer stand in its way, only small or weak nations teeming with resources. With the US policeman in retirement, why not?

China is not a nation but an empire of many peoples, languages. The dominance of the Han is greatly exaggerated. The Han are diverse peoples with different dialects and languages, many of them conquered peoples who have been acculturated but retain distinctive identities. Throughout China most people identify themselves first with their province or ethnic group, second with China. There is little love lost between them. The best hope for the rest of the world is a weakening of the center, a loosening of the ties.

There is a prospect that the binding element of the Mandarin writing system is doomed. China's script, even its language, is obsolete. Entry into the modern world has added a very large number of new foreign words which could not be practically introduced as new characters, but are written phonetically. The usual procedure is to select characters that replicate the sound of the foreign word, syllable by syllable. The Chinese already use phonetics in learning to read. More important is the universality of new communication technology. Writing Mandarin characters on cell phones, computers, etc. is extremely cumbersome and time consuming or next to impossible. Pin-yin – Chinese written in Roman letters – is widely used on computers. Users will become accustomed to communicating phonetically. They will gradually lose their competence in character reading and writing, and many in the next generation will never learn. Chinese languages and dialects will be printed in Roman letters, ending the imperialism of Mandarin.

The language itself is constrained by its script. There is a shortage of abstract words and of the connecting, relating, qualifying terms that permit the precision required for communication in a scientific society. It must evolve.

The people of China are not content with its traditional culture of authority and submission. Think of 1989 and Chinese students erecting a copy of the Statue of Liberty in Tiananmen Square. Starting even before with Sun-Yat sen some of its leaders have looked to the West for models, whether Jefferson, Montesquieu, or Marx, and now Adam Smith. The last Emperor is dead. On its borders, South Korea and Taiwan have undergone a cultural as well as economic revolution. Too many Chinese have traveled abroad and seen another world. The Emperor has been replaced by a committee of ten, whose reign is limited to ten years. The people have no trust in their government, in their leaders, and not much respect, just fear.

A nation no longer sharing a common script, unless it is phonetic, nor a common language, written or spoken, could evolve into another Europe, numerous semi-autonomous regions, some verging on independence, or at least into a federation like the United States, which is plural, not singular. Such a development would spare us the prospect of large scale warfare by an authoritarian state that does not recognize human rights or place much value on human life. What is required is a reversal of the direction of authority and representation from top down to bottom up, from dictatorship to democracy. Some progress in that direction is inevitable as China shifts from export-led growth to stress on domestic consumption, to economic democracy.

Of lower probability is Russian nostalgia for some of its former colonies and Javanese ambition to extend its oil resources and deforestation practices to all of Borneo and New Guinea.

Islamic Violence

Islamic terrorism ranges from suicide bombers to terrorist nations. Terrorists all because their common objective is murder. What else do they have in common? They come from oil-rich nations and dirt-poor nations; from nations with high unemployment and nations that import much of their labor force. Many are educated, some have lived long in Western nations. Their common objective is to kill Westerners whoever they are, wherever they can. The early 19th century Luddists destroyed the machines that had taken over their jobs. There was some rationality – perhaps they could have their old jobs back. But the Islamic Luddists display no such rationality. It matters little whom they kill, the body count is paramount. What they hope to accomplish is not clear. Perhaps some paranoid grandiose leaders think that societies will collapse and they can take over and restore Islam to dominance just because many unbelievers have been murdered. The targets are mostly targets of opportunity and of maximum destruction, not core facilities or infrastructure; cement does not bleed. The common aim seems to be destruction pure and simple. And the only shared characteristic is Islam.

Islamic authoritarianism, Islamic terrorism is an affliction of tribal cultures. Islam is a tribal religion. It shares a dual code of ethics – one for members of the tribe, for believers, another for nonmembers, for infidels. Any rights are restricted to members of the tribe or the faith. There is some looking backward to the glory days of Islamic conquest and civilization but mainly in the Arab world. There is envy and resentment of Western power and affluence and influence. It is a war against Western civilization, its values and its success. In particular it is a war against human rights, which are ecumenical.

Human rights: liberation of women, a secular impartial legal system, democracy, would destroy the authoritarian structure of their tribal society. It is a war to preserve authority and self-esteem. For many but not all, it is a matter of social as well as individual self-esteem. It is a choice for destruction over emulation. The only human "right" they all respect is the right of revenge.

Most Islamic nations are themselves divided. Most of the war against the west will be fought within Islamic nations, as we see today, where different denominations of Islam murder each other as well as the infidels among them, the secularists who wish to be part of western civilization. For Islamic nations it is a tragedy; for the advanced world, a nuisance, until the day some militant group buys a nuclear device from North Korea, which will sell anything it has to the highest bidder, or from Pakistan. I do not believe that most citizens of Islamic countries are participants or proponents of violence, they are not part of the problem, just the primary victims.

How long can this last? The supply of suicide bombers is finite; surveillance technology is improving. But rule by bullet instead of ballot could last out the century.

Not all members of militant groups, organizations are religious fanatics. Especially in poor countries, in Africa, many participants seek income, affluence, and some of its leaders are kleptocrats. They share the characteristics of the drug organizations of Central and South America. Killing and looting go hand in hand. Drug sales, kidnapping for ransom, help finance operations as well as enrich participants.

AFRICAN TURMOIL

Islamic militants apart, only Africa is in a state of constant warfare. With fertility rates of 4 and 5, its population is exploding, famine would be a permanent large scale feature but for foreign aid. Public health has cut down infant, child and maternal mortality rates. The Mediterranean rim nations aside, only South Africa ad Botswana have fertility close to a sustainable rate. The continent cannot feed itself, it is destroying the environment in its search for resources and agricultural land. There are kleptocratic governments, and resistance groups that seek to replace them in several nations.

Much of the continent is tribal in social organization, and still territorial, as the process of urbanization lags far behind that of Islamic nations. Fighting over territory or control comes naturally. There are always refugee problems. Famine, disease, refugees, warfare are an ethical problem for outsiders. In the northern part of the continent the economic struggle for survival is entangled with strife between religions.

Only Africans can help themselves. Rising dependency rates in the developed world as well as more serious threats to their security will limit their ability and their willingness to continue aid indefinitely. The World Bank has tried for over 60 years, but many countries are no better off now than they were at its inception, just more populated. Discoveries of oil may have done more than all the aid efforts of the developed world. Yes, development and urbanization bring down fertility rates, but the continent cannot wait. Fertility must drop to replacement levels or the four horsemen will deal with the population problem.

The problems of this century are global. Population growth and the struggle for affluence are straining the limits of the possible. Global policies for resource supply and distribution are required, but there is no global organization, no global power. Either a Malthusian solution, or a Darwinian.

Chapter 32

PAST AND FUTURE HISTORY

What does the history of the past two centuries tell us about prospects for the next? This could be a lifetime project for a historian. The past may influence but cannot determine the present or future; if it did one would imply an uncaused cause, in the realm of theology rather than history. The present is shaped by the past, but the future is not. History cannot tell us what to do, although it can warn us not to repeat some of the errors committed by our predecessors.

Most major events of the past two centuries have been driven by science or technology, directly or indirectly. Science and technology are evolutionary, not repetitive. In the presence of novelty, history cannot provide a basis for predicting the future. Perhaps before the scientific and industrial revolutions history might have been repetitive often, but not since. What we can learn from experience of a different past is limited. The closest we can come to repetition is analogy.

The human brain has not changed, but the mind has improved. Most of the world has become literate in the past 2 centuries. Literate people have much larger vocabularies – cognitive resources – than illiterates. Their thinking is more coherent and precise. This evolution is nearly over, but another is beginning. Whereas most intelligence tests show no trend, quantitative scores are rising. People are being flooded with numbers, exposed to graphs and tables as never before, and are improving their understanding of reality, probability, uncertainty.

A major consequence of science and technology has been a sextupling of world population. It will not be continued. The prospect now is of eventual decline, which has no historical precedent since the Toba volcanic explosion some 73,000 years ago. But growth has brought about further change. The culture of the 19th and early twentieth centuries was belief in progress and economic growth; now and for this century it is concern with environmental impacts of that growth: pollution, climate change, resource depletion and costs. The influence of the past is not creation of the present, but causation of potential effects. But historical causation is not determinism; cause and effect are intermediated by numerous factors. Single causes and single effects do not imply each other.

Another culture change refers to society and politics. A big issue prior to the past two centuries was the separation of church and state, a permanent achievement in the West, but still an issue in the Islamic world. Secular societies and peoples are new in human history, and there is no reason to believe that the process can be reversed next century by any theological faith. In the past century the political issue was secular: separation of economy and state, the conflict between capitalism and socialism (Marxism). In most of the world the issue is settled: separation. The globalization of the economy strongly favors the capitalist organization of production and distribution. But decline in growth will exacerbate the struggle for scarce resources between the economy and the state. Their relation may shift from complementary to competitive. The conflict of the next century is between society and the state, or representative democracy, and authoritarianism.

The age of empire is almost over. The number of nations, of independent actors on the world stage, has multiplied. Whether current efforts at regional integration will reduce their number to manageable size is yet to be seen. If there still remains an overseas empire, it is Java over Indonesia. But this is not a threat to world order. The overland empires are Russia and China. The current regime in Russia is nostalgic for its former empire, especially for the Trans-Caucasus- and the Ukraine, particularly the Crimea. It is not clear that the Russian people share such nostalgia. The most serious threat to world order is China, whose concept of its political and economic boundaries is in sharp conflict with those of other surrounding nations and which is clearly preparing for offensive action.

There is also the growing threat of nuclear, biological or chemical attacks by terrorist groups and nations. Pakistan, Iran, and North Korea are the leading threats, in that order. But the threat is criminal, not systemic. This is another byproduct of science and technology which did not exist in the past.

The past century has witnessed the nearly universal spread of the forms of democracy, but much less growth of the substance and the practices of human rights which are its foundation. This progress is under threat in a future of slower growth and possible decline. Democracy is well suited to share the gains of growth, but not the costs and losses of decline. Since democracy itself is responsible for excessive entitlements (but not for the fertility decline that made entitlements unaffordable), it may be said that democracy has become self-limiting. Income distribution will become the dominant political issue, one ill-suited for democratic solution in a century of diminished expectations and likely decline.

Most of the major historical events of the past two centuries are without precedent and unlikely to be replicated. The changes are self-limiting or have end-states. Science and technology alone appear to be open-end, short of reaching the limits of the human mind.

On science and technology, the 19th century was largely the domain of individuals, but the 20th was dominated by organized research. Thus the pace and direction of research has come under social control. The linkage of scientific knowledge and technological problem-solving has made the direction, the trajectory of progress more predictable. But it has also become more complex and costly. We do not know the future pace of technological progress, nor can we predict how breakthroughs will be used and incorporated in society. Discovery of laws of nature is even less subject to prediction. History invalidates our models.

Chapter 33

FAREWELL TO AFFLUENCE

INTRODUCTION

Industrial nations in the 20th century advanced rapidly in income per capita, grew wealthy. Their progress was driven by science and technology: electricity, communication, information, power, motor vehicles; by mass production and economies of scale. But the only nations that joined the club of wealthy developed countries during the century were Japan, South Korea and Taiwan (plus two city-states). They raised income per capita largely through sustained periods of very rapid growth in exports. But their combined population added less than 20% to the membership of the club. In the 21st century, China alone, growing at double digit rates until recently, exceeds the total population of the advanced nations club, and India comes close. The 21st century faces limits to export-led growth, and increasing pressure of demand on existing resources, renewable and nonrenewable alike. In combination with demographic changes they threaten to lower incomes of wealthy nations and impose a ceiling on the growth of developing nations.

The golden age of affluence came first to the United States because it came out of WWII with its economy intact. It came later to Western Europe and Japan, much later to Eastern Europe. The freeing of international trade gave it a boost. So did an increase in the ratio of the labor force to population. It continued uninterrupted to the present Great Recession. An earlier start, around the beginning of the 20th century, had been interrupted by two world wars and the Great Depression. But now the growth of underdeveloped nations, assisted by foreign aid and freer trade, is bringing affluence to an end.

This is the long term future. In the near term, many if not most nations must adjust to a combination of increased longevity and decreased fertility exerting downward pressure on incomes.

Demographic Depression

Fertility

Malthus is moribund. This is Margaret Sanger Day. Given our new ability to control reproduction, and the nearly world-wide trend to reduce it, population growth is no longer a threat in most nations; it is decline and its consequences that is a growing concern today. Our levels of living, not to mention those of most European nations, seem doomed to decline.

Population grew rapidly almost everywhere during most of the 20th century. But by its end, growth rates were declining almost everywhere, and falling fertility rates portend a decline in population in most of the developed world and, with a lag, in much of the underdeveloped world as well. Among advanced nations, fertility in the United States is just below replacement (or below, if the recession fertility decline persists), it is below replacement everywhere else except Israel. In Asia, India is still slightly above replacement, and Pakistan well above. All other large nations are at or below replacement. So are the larger nations in the Western Hemisphere. Only in Africa (except for the countries facing the Mediterranean and South Africa and Botswana) is fertility well above replacement rates, but falling.

The timing was right for the developed world: first they attained a high standard of living, and then they stabilized their population. The under-developed world, Africa excepted, is experiencing a dramatic decline in fertility and the prospect of population decline while still low income.

Nations with birth rates below 2.1 face current or eventual decline in population. This is true of all European nations. Of the larger nations, only the UK and France have fertility close to replacement; it is much lower for Germany, Italy, Spain and Russia. In the Western Hemisphere, all the larger nations: the U.S, Canada, and Brazil. Argentina, Mexico, Colombia have fertility at or below replacement. So do the large Muslim nations: Turkey, Iran, Bangladesh, Indonesia. Only Pakistan and Egypt have fertility significantly above replacement. Elsewhere in Asia, China, Japan and other East Asian nations have fertility far below replacement. India is slightly above, as are the Philippines, Thailand and Myanmar are below. Africa is another story. Of the 40 nations with fertility rates above 4, 38 are in Africa, including the largest, Nigeria. (Nations with high infant and maternal mortality or a high ratio of males to females need a fertility rate higher than 2.1 to maintain population.)

Such low fertility rates are without historical precedent. The conditions promoting them are without historical precedent. The trend in all cases has been downward; we do not know how long or how far it will continue. Major causal factors include birth control technology and urbanization. Since fertility declined in nations already heavily urbanized, its decline in developing nations cannot be explained mainly in terms of urbanization. Nor is the decline limited to urban areas. Public policies and parental motivation to raise school-leaving age and public policies raising the minimum working age all increase the costs of child rearing. A further factor is the educational and occupational opportunities for women. The spread of retirement pensions, as well as health insurance, reduce the dependence of the elderly on support from their children.

There is no reason to believe that the major causal factors will cease to operate in the extended future. Nor do we have policies effective in counteracting their consequences. But nations subject to the same causal factors have differences in fertility rates, as they did in the past. Values, motives, preferences differ, and they are subject to change from one generation to another.

Longevity

The decline in fertility has been accompanied by an increase in life expectancy. Most of the increase in longevity in affluent countries until late into the 20th century was attributable to reductions in infant mortality. In the United States it declined from 100 per thousand in 1900 to 29 in 1950 largely as a result of public health and sanitation, and to 7 in 2000. In the last half of the century the antibiotic revolution and other medical advances escalated life expectancy of the population over 60 and especially over 80 years old. Life expectancy roughly doubled in the last century.

In underdeveloped nations there was less lag between these two contributors to longevity. And both came at an earlier stage of economic development. As a result the ratio of workers to population is declining almost simultaneously in rich countries and many poor countries alike.

Dependency Ratio

Per capita income, and the prospects for its growth, is affected by the ratio of workers to non-workers. Low fertility implies that each successive generation is smaller than its predecessor. This means a declining ratio of workers to non-workers, since it is the larger generations that retire first. The primary result is that income per capita increases less, or decreases more, than income per worker.

The dependency ratio is conventionally defined as number of persons under age 15 plus the number over age 64, divided by the number aged 15-64. But the cost of children dependents is an investment in future labor, whereas the cost of elderly dependents is not. It is a crude approach to the ratio of workers to non-workers, useful in making international comparisons.

Demographically, it is the ratio of age group numbers that matters. The burden of dependency can be reduced. In fact working age has been rising, both legally and in terms of entry delayed by rising educational attainment. Retirement age is also subject to change legally and in fact is increasing in many countries. As to the working age population, what matters is labor force participation. This has risen markedly for women. But changes in female labor force participation are inversely correlated with birth rates. Stay-at home moms are workers too, not dependents.

Nations can influence the ratio of workers to non workers for a given age distribution. Differences in female labor force participation are a matter of culture, training, and child care responsibilities. Nurseries, daycare centers can free mothers for the labor force. Training can improve employment choices. Nations must consider the desirability of delaying the age of entry into the labor force by prolonging the education of most young people.

But the most important difference in practice is retirement age, from Greece, 50 for women and 55 for men, to the United States, over 66, rising to 67 for social security eligibility, and absence of any compulsory retirement age for most occupations and many employers. A long working life lightens the burden on workers of paying for the entitlements of the elderly. They have more years during which to contribute, fewer during which to receive pensions and other benefits. The number of hours worked per year ranges from less than 1,500 to over 2,000 among advanced nations. It is another means of increasing the labor force. Benefits may also be reduced by making the amount inversely related to income of the recipient.

A nation in demographic decline that does not utilize some of these options will spiral down to bankruptcy as more and more of its young workers emigrate, reshaping the age pyramid.

Estimating future trends in the dependency ratio involves two basic assumptions: fertility and longevity. We simply do not know their future, but assume that fertility rates will remain constant, and that longevity will increase slowly. Those who will be retiring in the 2070s have already been born. The largest unknown is the fertility trends of underdeveloped nations whose fertility is still quite high, although declining in nearly every case. Most of them are in Africa. The entitlement revolution, education and health care in particular, is arriving earlier in the stage of development of the third world than it did in the first. Governments may find it difficult to finance both physical and human investment.

What are the implications of a high and rising dependency ratio driven by increased longevity? Nearly all advanced nations, and some not so advanced, have taxpayer-financed government programs subsidizing the cost of health care for the aged. Most also have government retirement pensions. Procedures vary, but in many cases they are, or will be, paid from current tax revenues. A rise in dependency ratio increases the burden to workers of benefits for the retired. It means higher tax revenues paid by a shrinking workforce to subsidize a growing population of retirees.

The increase in dependency ratio does not take into account some associated increases in the cost of living of the very elderly, paid in part by workers. Many who would have died earlier are kept alive by modern technology at considerable expense. Many more join assisted living facilities, involving either some support from the working population or reduction in distribution from the elderly to the next generation. When the elderly had more children and close relatives, they were likely to share a household with family members at much lower cost.

The share of the economy financed by taxation is too high in most developed countries. It is too high in part because of the growing burden of entitlements. An increase in the tax burden beyond some point deters enterprise, investment, economic growth. If it is one third, then the tax on the non-government sector is 50%, with no tax exemptions for private sector schools, churches, hospitals. It would initiate a spiral of economic decline. Even with 25% of the economy tax-financed, the average rate on the remainder would be 33%. In comparing tax burdens across nations, one needs to keep in mind that the range of government functions varies widely between nations. If government, not the private sector, pays for health care, college education, it needs a larger tax base than if these remain in the private sector, and the economy can bear a higher burden without counterproductive effects on investment and growth.

There is also the looming prospect of surplus housing and surplus of many very durable goods as population declines. The surplus could reduce cost of living, but employment in these industries would decline.

The Baby Bubble and the Next Generation

As a result of the great depression followed by WWII, the postwar baby boom generation in the United States was much bigger than its predecessor. But succeeding generations were smaller, as fertility rates fell. While this generation was growing up there was a "bubble" in school enrollments; when it reached working age there was a "bubble' in the labor force, reducing the dependency ratio. Now that "bubble" is moving out of the labor force into retirement, with higher life expectancy than its predecessors. It will be replaced in the labor force by smaller generations. Until it is mostly gone from this world the dependency ratio will be high, depressing per capita incomes.

For the United States this could be a temporary problem, until the baby boomers are gone. Pre-recession fertility rates were just below replacement levels. Should current lower fertility return to pre-recession levels, the dependency ratio will only increase to the extent that longevity rises among the elderly. Fertility rates will likely remain somewhat below replacement, but population may not decline, given continuing net in-migration.

For most other developed nations the dependency ratio will continue to rise, since their fertility rates are well below replacement rate. Each succeeding generation entering the labor force will be smaller than its predecessor.

Nearly all developed nations and many others face continuing decline in total population without a large continuing inflow of migrants. Most migration today is from poor countries to rich ones by young working age adults, lowering the dependency ratio in the country of destination, raising it in the country of origin. But most rich nations find it very difficult to assimilate migrants and are reluctant to follow this route. Globally, the need for immigrants to avoid population decline and dependency ratio increase will rise, but the supply of immigrants could decline, as the numbers in the age-group most likely to emigrate keeps falling.

China, India and other developing nations are confronting changes more abrupt than those confronting Europe. Large increases in longevity of the population 65 and over can be expected, as they converge on the developed world. School-leaving age will rise considerably in countries many of whose children do not finish elementary school, most do not go beyond it. The dependency ratio is likely to rise more than in advanced nations, and while they are still low-income. Urbanization itself is a process that increases dependency.

DEVELOPMENT AND DISTRIBUTION

The Affluent Few

The developed high income world of North America, most European nations, Australia, New Zealand. Japan, Taiwan, South Korea. and Singapore total roughly a billion people, a small proportion of world population. It was possible for Taiwan and South Korea to achieve European levels of income by export-led growth; their economies are small compared to world trade. It was barely possible for Japan to do the same, with the aid of highly protectionist policies and given its already high level of industrialization. It may be possible for Russia and Brazil because their growth need not be import-dependent; they are resource-rich. It is not possible for China or India.

Timing is important for growth. Demographic transition constrains the prospects of late-developing nations in lifting per capita income. The first nations to industrialize did so while birth rates were high and life expectancy was low. The ratio of working age population to total population was high. Working age started much younger then than it does now. Even those nations that achieved affluence in the 20th century did so before fertility rates plunged, leading to reduction of the labor force, with a lag, and before large increases of their elderly population.

Today most industrializing nations have already experienced large declines in fertility, which is well below replacement rate in the case of China and Russia. The decline in labor force is imminent, the ratio of elderly to working population is already increasing, long before per capita income comes close to that of the nations that succeeded in the 19th and 20th centuries. With fertility below 2.1 and increasing longevity, this ratio will continue declining for much of the 21st century.

Empire and the Industrial Revolution

The leading industrial nations of the 19th and 20th centuries were all overseas empires. Long before the Industrial Revolution, Spain and Portugal led the way in empire-building, soon followed by the English, French, and Dutch. Overseas empires supplied cheap resources and labor, and in some cases captive markets. The British, French and Dutch did not lose most of their empires until just after WWII. Portugal and Spain lost most of theirs in the 19th century, one reason for their lagging behind. Germany and Italy did not become unified nations until the 19th century, their empires were late, small, and brief; so was Belgium's. Japan built its empire starting in the 1890s which lasted for no more than two generations. But post-imperial Japan was surrounded by nations with huge supplies of very cheap labor and natural resources. During a more recent period it benefited from falling trade barriers and cheap transport.

The United States had a brief fling at empire, but it never relied on foreign resources or cheap foreign labor for its growth, one reason it has out-performed other industrial nations in recent decades. Its empire, its resources, were predominantly internal. Immigrant labor was always available.

All of these nations, the United States Canada and Australia excepted, were or became resource-poor in terms of their population and the requirements of the industrial age. Germany developed alternative sources of competitive advantage, technology in particular. Beyond the reach of empire, Europe and Japan (and the United States to a lesser extent) benefited from cheap labor in underdeveloped nations and cheap imports of production resources: fuels, minerals, and agricultural products, as well as low-skill labor-intensive consumer goods.

Today the cost of labor in the developing world is rising with growth, and so is the cost of other productive resources for all nations. Developing nations such as China greatly increase their demand for imported oil, minerals, and agricultural products. Nations that are themselves exporters, such as Brazil and Indonesia, will consume more of their surpluses domestically, and charge more for exports.

Supply Constraints

China's per capita income has risen to about one eighth of our own. There is no way it can ever come close to European levels. But the effort to do so will bring down living levels in all major advanced nations and lower standards in much of the rest of the world. China plus India are one third of world population. Their combined demand for the resources required to maintain high growth must drive up prices.

It should be stressed that the problem of supply is not primarily one of population. Population is growing more slowly than in the 20th century, at a pace compatible with technological change. It is the growth of per capita demand that is proceeding in a time frame too short for technological solutions.

Why should a rapid increase in the demand for resources be self-limiting? It is not just the depletion of stocks of nonrenewable goods that will drive up costs - that is a long run prospect; which might be mitigated by technological change. It is the shorter run rapid increase in demand for resources, renewable or not, that tends to exceed supply and lead to higher-cost expansion of output, slowing income growth. Already the prices of crude oil and of numerous ocean fish have soared.

For many critical items expansion of world supply to keep up with rapidly rising demand can only come at increasing costs. Lower grade minerals, deeper mines will be exploited. Poorer lands will be cultivated, and existing lands will be cultivated more intensively. For many goods that are renewable or reproducible, increase in supply takes much time. Some forest products take many years to grow to harvest size. Increasing forest harvesting rates to meet demand may simply reduce stocks, limiting supplies and driving up prices in the future. Opening up new lands for cultivation involves investments in infrastructure: transportation, power, communication. It also removes lands from other uses. Construction of new manufacturing capacity requires time.

The oceans are being over-fished. The annual catch of most species desired as food for humans, notably cod, salmon, tuna, exceeds the fertility rate of the species; stocks are declining. Ocean fishery catch on a sustainable basis is not sufficient to meet demand today, much less if much of the world becomes customers. Higher-cost fish farming is a growth industry.

Life in the oceans is an extremely complex structure of predator and prey. It should be viewed as a network of food chains, with man as the top predator. The annual catch of any species will have repercussions throughout the system. There is no equilibrium of species and numbers.

There is no consensus on targets or goals. The Japanese would want a monopoly of blue fin tuna; the Americans prefer salmon, lobster, ban whales. Koreans love eel. Even if there were agreement on goals, how could they be monitored and enforced and by whom? Most ocean fish are caught in international waters. No nation has the right, responsibility, or resources to patrol, inspect, enforce any limits on catch on a regional scale, never mind global. Not all nations will close their ports to forbidden catch.

Forests too are being over-harvested. The supply of ebony wood from Africa, once used for piano keys among other uses, of Pernanbuco wood from Brazil, preferred for violin bows, and many other forest products, have been depleted to the brink of extinction, their prices have soared. Cypress forests of the American South have been converted to telephone poles across the land. These "crops" take many years to grow.

At least a billion people obtain more than half their calories from rice. Probably another billion` are equally dependent on maize, manioc, potatoes. These are crops with a very high calorie yield per acre. As incomes rise, this dependence will diminish. Feeding grains to animals that are then eaten is a much less efficient use of land. People will obtain their calories farther up the food chain: meat, milk, cheese, eggs. Meat may require five times the land area per calorie of the high yield grain and root crops. Reduced calorie productivity of land in food and feed crops increases pressure on land supply and costs, not just in food and feed crops, but also in industrial crops competing for land use. Only agricultural research has prevented a decline in agricultural yields, as much Midwest topsoil now lines the bottom of the Gulf of Mexico.

Shifting from grains and tubers to animal products, or even to leafy vegetables, carrots, tomatoes, eggplant, asparagus, fruits will mean a large decline in the calorie productivity of agricultural land. There is no hope that research can significantly narrow the gap in calorie productivity of grain and meat. Calories are not the only consideration, but they are essential for survival.

Ergo, the long term trend of a declining share of income spent on food could be reversed. The shift in diet is not just to lower-calorie yield foods, but to higher cost of production foods. Rising costs of production would counteract any increase in incomes. The level of sustainability will depend on choice of menus, in particular the shift from vegetable food to animal meat and byproducts.

The stock of agricultural land can be reduced, or its productivity downgraded, by overuse, improper use: monoculture, erosion. salination. It can be expanded, at the cost of pasture, forest, or swamp. It can be created in some places by chemical or mechanical engineering: fertilizers and other soil additives, terracing, drainage. Agricultural output is sustainable only subject to constraints of land, water, and climate. Progress in agro-biology will be major determinants of what is possible.

Rainfall can be supplemented by irrigation from rivers and lakes, whose supply is constantly being replenished. It can be increased by water mining. Whatever the source of water, agriculture competes with urban and industrial demands. It is also possible to modify plants genetically to require less water, as well as shift to crops that need less water. Seawater can be desalinated, at a high price. Waste water can be cleansed.

Climate is another constraint on agricultural land and output. Warming extends the range within which certain crops may be grown, and moves the boundaries of agriculture pole-ward and upward. It may also mean loss of some land formerly used or usable for agriculture, whether from desiccation or ocean flooding. There is not much we can do about climate, but geneticists can help plants adapt, and farmers can change crop mix.

Some developing nations are exploiting their renewable resources well above replacement rates. China in particular must divert investment to counteract the consequences of staggering levels of pollution of air, water and soil. The stock whence comes the flow is being destroyed; soil does not renew itself.

Estimating the costs and limits of non-renewable resource production is another matter. There is some fungibility of demands: oil, gas, coal, wood, steel, stone, cement, plastic – and some of supplies. It is the hydrocarbons that concern us, whether as fuels or as raw materials.

China, India

The growth of some developing nations, China in particular, faces an additional problem. Their rapid growth is based mainly on export to other countries. Some nations have attained a population and income level that is unsustainable without large imports and therefore export dependence to pay for imports. This was true of a number of high income nations in the 20th century, notably Japan, but also Hong Kong, Singapore, South Korea, Taiwan. It had been true earlier of most European nations, and remains true today. But they were a small proportion of world population. Import (and export) dependent growth of low income nations in the current century requires an enormous growth in world imports and exports that is not forthcoming. China and India combined account for one third of world population.

China until recently was growing at a 10% annual rate by exporting 39% of its GDP, an incredibly large share for such a big country (The U.S. exports only 12% of its GDP, Japan 15%.). Its exports quintupled between 2000 and 2009; it now accounts for more than 10% of world exports. If it were to maintain this rate of growth, by the end of the decade it would account for some 40% of world exports, assuming that the latter grow 25%. It would also account for 30% of world imports, assuming the same ratio of exports to imports in 2020 which prevailed in 2009. This is over. China's exports in 2012 were down to 30% of GDP, and its imports to 26%, and bound to decline further. The growth of world demand for exports will slow down for two reasons: first, economic growth rates will be lower as long as dependency rates are rising; and much of the decline in tariffs and other trade barriers, and in transport costs, is behind us.

We can forecast the future of China by reviewing the history of Japan. Japanese GDP grew five-fold between 1953 and 1970, or roughly 10% a year. Growth then dropped to the 4-5% range for a while, then to 2% or less. But it had attained first world levels of living. China will not be able to replicate this achievement. In the first place, it started far behind Japan in income and technological capability. In the second place, its population is ten times that of Japan. It is saturating export markets, facing increasing labor costs at home and competition from other nations at a level of GDP per capita far below that of Japan's at a similar stage. Another difference in historical context is that Japan grew rapidly when no other large nation was doing likewise. China should be able to maintain fairly rapid growth longer than Japan, because its lag in technology, human capital, and infrastructure was much greater than Japan's.

China must restructure its economy to reduce trade dependence and rely on domestic demand for self-sustaining growth. Its competitive advantage is declining, and some markets are saturated. Its import requirements drive up costs. The large gains in productivity from catching up are diminishing. The huge gap between the value of China's exports and the value of its imports is also unsustainable, as well as incompatible with free trade. China's growth policies will have to undergo radical and risky changes. Growth in domestic consumption will have to substitute for export growth. But this would require an increase in the share of GDP going to wages and consumed, a decline in the share invested, a decline in government power and control from the center. A consumption-driven economy cannot be planned. Producing for domestic markets will require continued import of raw materials and other inputs which must be paid for. Relative to its population, China is resource=poor

The Chinese government has managed to prolong the period of rapid growth by limiting domestic consumption through a combination of low wages and absence of a social safety net. Now the labor force will decline as a consequence of the low birth rates of the past three decades, the dependency ratio will zoom. Wages must continue to rise. As the population urbanizes and ages, a social safety net must be built and financed.

India at this point is far less export-dependent and slower growth. But soon it will have more people than China; it could replicate China's recent trajectory until mid-century. It is better endowed with agricultural land, it is less resource-deficient, and faces a smaller decline in the ratio of labor force to population in the decades ahead. But it also is too big to depend on exports of manufactures for long as a major source of growth, and likely too late, given China's market share. It will be a big exporter of services, which require few imported resources, much investment in human capital.

It is not possible to triple the number of affluent population this century. The average level of affluence itself will be under downward pressure from the effort to increase the total number. Think of the consequences of quadrupling Chinese GDP per capita, to still well below European standards, in terms of energy requirements, cars on the road, fuel needs, import demands, export earnings. The supply of needed imports does not exist, and is unlikely ever to exist for many resources except at growth-reducing costs, if at all.

Resource-rich nations, such as Brazil and Russia, should have an easier time maintaining growth long enough to attain affluence. They do not have so far to go. In fact neither Russia nor Brazil need rely heavily on exports for growth; they are capable of self-sustaining growth. The large exporters of agricultural and mineral products may experience economies of scale in production, as well as sale at rising prices.

Resource Wars

There are two ways for a resource-poor nation to maintain rapid growth. Post-WWII Japan and all the Asian tigers propelled growth through export promotion, as has China until now. The revenues from exports allowed them to pay for the imports needed to maintain rapid growth. This policy may work indefinitely for a small country, but only for a short time for a nation as large as Japan.

The second path was followed by Japan prior to and during World War II. It is a crowded nation, with limited level land and inadequate industrial resources relative to its population. I do not know the reasoning that persuaded the Japanese leaders that simply buying needed imports was not sufficient means of maintaining rapid growth. This was a day of high tariffs and other import impediments to trade; perhaps export-led growth was impossible in the longer run, or inadequate even in the shorter run. Perhaps Japan was concerned that the main sources of needed imports, in Southeast Asia, consisted almost entirely of colonies of the British, French, Dutch and Americans. It sought security of resources by waging war against the colonial powers and occupying their colonies. The colonies may also have been seen as potential markets. In the 1890s it had already occupied Korea and Taiwan, sources of cheap labor, and shortly before the war established dirty heavy industry in Manchuria.

Japan moved south, through the British, American, French and Dutch empires. It felt it had no alternative. China could follow the same route, eased by the elimination of empires. The territory was once policed by the Americans, who may no longer be on the job. Or it could move north into Siberia, confronting Russian nuclear weapons, and/or west into Central Asia. So far as oil and gas is concerned, import from the land-bound Central Asian nations is probably an acceptable policy. But Southeast Asia is much the richer prize in resources, labor, markets. This is the direction China is headed today. But as indicated earlier here is an alternative path.

China's supply of cheap labor has been essential but not much longer. Export growth will be slowing dramatically in the immediate future. To maintain rapid growth in output for domestic consumption rather than for exports. Wages must rise for consumption to grow. This resource-poor nation must import mineral and agricultural resources. Nor will it be self-contained in all consumer products or capital goods. Affluent Chinese wish to import real German cars, Swiss army knives or Leica cameras, instead of making do with the often shoddy domestic copies. They are buying baby food in Hong Kong. The lack of trust in Chinese products is widespread if not universal.

How will China pay for increasing imports if its export earnings are not increasing? One way is to buy the foreign supplying companies, assuring access to their output and perhaps paying below-market prices. It is doing this. But firms in another country subject to a different legal and political regime, is not a guarantee of control. The other alternative is to acquire the country rather than the firm, guaranteeing supply. Its land grabs so far from several adjoining nations cannot be described as resource raids, except for the conquest of Tibet.

Today we see China preparing to follow precisely in Japan's steps, not the post-WWII which led to affluence, but the pre-WWII which led to disaster. Its military buildup, especially its navy, cannot be explained in terms of defense against any potential attacker, only in terms of deterring interference. It must consider the cost of conquest and occupation vs. the cost of alternative means of obtaining needed supplies vs. the risks and costs of accepting a large slowdown in growth rates. Conquest may also be a means of acquiring a supply of very cheap labor once the domestic supply has been exhausted and domestic wages risen. The ultimate cost is the same as Japan's: that of deterring intervention by the United States.

Today one thinks of the potential for resource wars primarily as the search for oil in the South China Sea. Argentina is newly agitated about British control of the Falkland or Malvinas islands now that large oil finds are in prospect. Tomorrow there may be controversies over mineral rights in the Arctic Ocean.

Less noted are multiple international controversies over river water management between adjacent nations through which major rivers flow. Tomorrow climate change could promote water wars. The upstream country can control the flow of water and its volume. Flood control and navigation are in mutual interest, But flow control creates conflicts. Hydroelectric power means large reservoirs that reduce the total flow through upstream seepage and evaporation. But the greater issue is diversion of water for urban and industrial needs, for agricultural irrigation.

The major river systems that raise the question of to whom belongs the water are the Nile in Africa, the Tigris-Euphrates in the Middle East, the Syr Darya and Amur-Darya in Central Asia, and the rivers originating in the Himalayas and the Tibetan Plateau: the Indus, Ganges, Irrawaddy, and Mekong in particular.

Quite apart from human manipulation, the flow of some rivers varies from year to year and may change dramatically with climate change. All countries concerned could face a decline in water supply. Industrialization and urbanization increase demand, generating shortages even if flows are maintained. Then water wars would be more likely.

Limits to Growth

The pursuit of affluence is limited by three rules or laws: First, the invention/imitation cost ratio is high whether measured in cost or in time. The most advanced nations grow through invention and innovation, slowly and at great cost. Nations catching up can leapfrog all the intervening stages of development, copy instead of create. They can grow very rapidly for extended periods, as did Japan, South Korea, Taiwan, and now China.

The evidence is overwhelming. No advanced nation has ever grown year after year at double digit or high single-digit rates; several underdeveloped nations have. Advanced nations grow at high rates only for a year or two following some economic disaster: depression, war. It follows that many developing countries have narrowed the gap between themselves and the United States considerably, and continue to narrow the remaining gap.

Whereas the United States grows largely through research, development and invention, many developed nations, small ones in particular, grow largely by imitation. They grow slowly because their technological lag is small, they are not pole-vaulting several generations of technology at a time.

The cost of imitation and adoption has been lowered by free trade and international investment, the growth of multinational corporations and technology transfer. Education and training of workers in developing countries has enabled them to master new technologies. Meanwhile, the cost of invention in advanced nations keeps rising. The invention/imitation ratio is rising.

Second, the law of diminishing returns: At the enterprise level there are economies of scale. But at the global level they are diseconomies. Resources, renewable or not, vary in quality or accessibility. Expanded demand and production leads to use of higher-cost supplies. This happens in any case, but rapid growth accelerates the process. Research reduces the rate of depletion and/or cost increase, but it cannot stop it. Since matter cannot be created or destroyed, some nonrenewable productive resources can be recycled, others cannot. We will never run out of iron, it is such a large proportion of the earth. But scrap iron is rarely pure iron, rather rusted alloys, not all of it is worth collecting and recycling. Hydrocarbon fuels produce carbon dioxide in the atmosphere, absorbed by the oceans, consumed by plants. But the costs of recycling are much too high to be considered any time soon.

Before the industrial revolution, the British, and most other peoples, relied on renewable fuels and materials, namely wood. Wood was the main fuel, it was also the material used to build ships and carriages. But as forests were cut down, the UK ran out of naval timber. It was also running out of charcoal for iron-making, or finding it too costly. Fortunately it now possessed the American colonies which were able to supply the timber.

The Industrial Revolution changed all that, building ships and carriage of steel, not wood, and using coking coal instead of charcoal for producing iron. It shifted the economic base of society from potentially renewable to nonrenewable and eventually exhaustible materials and fuels. It also led to a population explosion in the twentieth century and a drive for higher incomes. For two centuries only a minority of world population experienced an industrial revolution, but now most of the remainder is catching up. We are now at the point of diminishing returns from our stock of some nonrenewable resources and must consider the consequences for levels of living and social structure.

This is not the future, it is the recent past. Earnings per full time employee peaked in 1970 and are lower today. We have grown in per capita income only because of a large increase in labor force participation by women, a higher ratio of workers to population than before. This is over, and with an aging population, the ratio of workers to population will continue declining..

Third, the fallacy of composition follows from the other two rules. What is true or possible for any one individual or nation is not necessarily possible for many and impossible for all. In its extreme form, anyone can be first, but not everyone, in fact only one can be first. The idea of the commons is a more diluted version: one person's behavior makes no difference; but as the number of agents increases, there is a "just noticeable difference" and eventually a transformation of the environment.

The high living standards of Western Europe were attainable because these nations were a small portion of world population and their depletion of domestic nonrenewable resources came early, when they could be readily supplemented by imports. The unintended consequences: their increased demand for the resources and labor of underdeveloped nations were on the whole beneficial for the supplier. North America was the exception, its growth was not dependent on foreign labor or imported resources.

The twentieth century marked a turning point. It combined a quadrupling of world population with an acceleration of economic growth. First came the rise of Japan to advanced nation, high living standards, a mixed blessing to older advanced nations: cheap imports on one hand, loss of jobs on the other. But the accelerated growth of China and India, one third of world population, has Malthusian consequences. We are not talking about starvation, disease, a la Malthus, but we do face a Malthusian fate nonetheless. Population must decline radically or standards of living in affluent nations decline as most of the population in the developing world becomes developed. To believe otherwise is to fall for the fallacy of composition.

What is the world population compatible with preservation of renewable resources? There is no one answer; for each resource the steady state population may be different. Further, technological change will change the numbers. Supposing we should all become vegetarians? Supposing we changed our housing practices if not preferences: fewer detached houses, more multi-generation family units, greater resort to communal rather than household facilities and services.

There are two key renewable resources whose supply exceeds any conceivable human need, at a cost. One is water, and the price is the desalinization of seawater. The other is energy derived from the sun, again at a current cost far exceeding that of hydrocarbon fuels. Other options remain glints in the minds eyes of physicists and engineers.

How rapidly water becomes an increasingly scarce resource depends largely on regional population trends. Some water is depletable: underground reservoirs of old geological origin. Water tables are declining almost everywhere. But ocean water is inexhaustible, at the cost of desalinization. Here the cost of energy becomes the determinant of the cost of water, which in turn becomes a major factor in the cost of food and other agricultural resources.

The ultimate resource is energy. The primary source, the base power, must be available 24 hours a day. Currently it is coal (nuclear in France). As the cost of coal rises, and that of natural gas falls, it might replace coal, but eventually its cost also will escalate as the most accessible supplies are exhausted. Bio fuels is too land-intensive, the total sustainable supply too small, apart from the fact that reliance on bio fuels will drive up the cost of food worldwide. It is an 18th century solution.

The base power could be nuclear, which will last out the millennium. Solar energy cannot replace it until such time that it can be stored for months at reasonable cost. This time may never come. A less unlikely possibility is electric cables circling the globe, delivering solar energy from wherever the sun is shining to wherever it is not. The cost of a calorie-driven man with hoe or a shovel sets an upper limit to the cost of alternative energy.

TOWARDS THE TWENTY SECOND CENTURY

Centuries are short if measured in generations. Millions now in kindergarten will still be alive early in the next century. The baby boom generation is beginning to retire. Population in this country and the globe will be growing for several decades, then global population will begin to shrink. But it still will be larger at the beginning of the 22nd century than it was at the beginning of the 21st.

Decline of Affluence

Affluence will decline faster or rise more slowly, than before, in all nations with fertility rates below replacement level of 2.1. The lower the rate, the greater the downward pressure on affluence. Increased longevity will also contribute. The basic reason is increase in dependency ratio: a decline in the proportion of the population of working age and working. In most developing countries this age-based increase in dependency will be supplemented by rise in age of entry into the labor force; as educational achievement rises from very low levels toward those characteristic of advanced nations. But low birth rates may raise the rate of female labor force participation in some of them. The other factor driving affluence down is rising prices of consumer goods driven by the demand of rapidly growing large nations, should China and India and other large nations still be growing in population or income which is doubtful (except for Nigeria in population). Rising labor costs in the large low-income nations as their labor force declines will also contribute to higher commodity prices. In this case there are winners as well as losers. Nations with large earnings from export of mineral and agricultural products could benefit. Nations whose growth is dependent on manufacturing exports are particularly vulnerable. Manufacturing is migratory; mines and farms are not.

The Future of Fertility

We cannot forecast how future generations will be motivated. The best we can do at this point is assume that recent birth rates will be maintained. The different assumption, that recent trends will be maintained, is impossible; it will lead eventually to zero population. The additional burdens imposed on workers for the next several generations by the rising dependency ratio are disincentives for procreation.

Over many generations, those adults with a preference for more children will people the next generation with their offspring. A question for research is whether the children from large families have more children than those from families with a single child. What is the relation between numbers of offspring in successive generations? At some future date this Darwinian process may outweigh the disincentives for procreation. Fertility will rise, the dependency ratio will fall. But this reasoning is more speculation than prediction. Nor can we predict the century or population level at which its decline will bottom out.

Another speculation refers to the nature of government in some countries. Nazi Germany had its baby factories. One can imagine some future government, such as China's today, converting its abortion clinics into fertility farms, under the law and with an element of compulsion in both cases.

Population Redistribution

If there is considerable global warming one can safely predict a northward movement of population – a peopling of the empty vastness of Siberia, the Canadian north, Baffin and other arctic islands, Alaska. In the Southern Hemisphere there is Patagonia, little else to open up short of Antarctica itself.

Many countries, mostly low-income, are over-populated in terms of their domestic resources, agricultural, industrial, and human. This could be another way of looking at export dependence for employment and growth in income. Export of people is one response. However, emigrants are likely to be working age, so that the solution could be worse than the problem.

No nation is likely to adopt a policy of reducing its population by half as a means of attaining high standards of living, even if the payoff were immediate instead of generations down the road. China's one child policy is the one example of an attempt to limit population growth more than as a means of reducing China's population. And its unintended consequences - sex imbalance, high dependency ratio - are leading to some reconsideration.

The policy many countries will consider, some are considering now, is increased in-migration to reduce the dependency ratio, and to avoid population decline. But this is a zero-sum game. The total number of immigrants may rise, but net in-migration and net out-migration are equal. Which nations are most likely to benefit? Migration tends to be from lower to higher income nations, and there is no reason to expect this to change. But among higher-income nations, which will be the greater gainers? Probably the most important consideration in the minds of immigrants is the subjective probability of finding employment.

Few nations have demonstrated an ability to integrate large numbers of different ethnicity and/or culture. So migration as a solution to high dependency ratios and declining population is a high social cost strategy.

Today most countries impose limits on immigration. They discriminate in terms of occupation, assets, country of origin, numbers, kinship. If what they seek is workers, their criteria will bend toward that objective. But what about the right to emigrate? Most countries impose no restrictions. But some nations require official approval. Authoritarian governments typically have reservations about voting, including voting with one's feet.

Emigrants typically have moved for economic reasons from countries with high rates of unemployment and underemployment. Their governments were content to see them go. Their departure reduced the unemployment problem at home, and led to immigrant remittances. Dependency ratios were low. But if lower-income nations in the future have high dependency ratios, they may be reluctant to see young working age adults depart. The freedom to emigrate may become a human rights issue.

Some nations may still have high fertility rates, low incomes, and poor economic prospects. Here emigration is an issue not of individual rights, but of social ethics. Should wealthy nations with a need for workers continue to subsidize high fertility and overpopulation by foreign aid and absorb the surplus workers?

Technological Salvation?

The industrial revolution is over. So much has been accomplished in productivity gains that what remains may seem trivial by comparison. Ah, but research will solve all problems. Many people believe in miracles, but the nature of miracles is that they cannot be predicted. In this instance we are praying for research to increase productivity by a large factor in a large number of research areas in the near future: food, energy, materials. We are assuming that invention will be cheap and that creativity is an assembly line that yields a product on demand and on schedule. The concept of an R&D production function is a figment of MBA imagination.

The technological and scientific advances of the 20th century may not have been possible without the enormous increase in scientists and engineers. The 21st will experience a further large increase in the numbers in the occupations that generate most of our new knowledge and new technology.

Numbers are needed but they are not enough. There are two components of performance: the first is schooling. The quality of public education in a nation is only part of the story. Mastery of math and science is not the same thing as the creativity required for discovery and much invention. The second component is the culture in which the graduates will work. Think of the Soviet Union, and its successor, Russia, a very large country, with many gifted scientists and engineers. But the only technological contribution that comes to mind is the AK-47. Tiny Israel outperforms the entire Muslim world. A culture that seeks novelty, that is future-oriented, capable of taking risks, favors discovery and invention. One that is nostalgic, backward-looking, averse to change, inhibits progress. Authoritarianism is the enemy no. 1 of creativity. A culture of deference, obedience and tradition is enemy no. 2. Democracy is not a culture of creativity per se but it allows it. The uncertain fate of democracy is closely linked to the future of discovery and invention.

The United States was dominant in the 20th century in science and technology, but a disproportionate contribution came from foreign-born immigrants. This dominance will diminish but not disappear, as long as its culture and infrastructure attracts the most gifted discoverers and inventors from across the world. The East Asian nations that do so well in education have quite different cultures, that value stability, certainty, tradition. India is more promising than East Asia because of its tradition of deductive reasoning and practice of argument and debate, that is a complicated story not to be told here. But it lacks the infrastructure and the culture of innovation.

The amount of knowledge that must be mastered by potential discoverers and inventors has multiplied, but the human brain is no better than before the industrial revolution. In many fields the easy discoveries and inventions have been made. What was once the work of individuals has become the research of large teams and costly instruments. The cost of invention has been rising. There is some suspicion that the productivity of research and development, however measured, has been falling. This is true of pharmaceutical research; antibiotics and bacteria are nearly stalemated. Much of the new technology of recent decades has little or no effect on productivity. It contributes to the quality of life, enhancing the capacity for consumption and its quality. Diminishing returns in this century are to be expected. What new technological trajectories may be launched this century, and to what ends, no one knows.

Technological change involves both generation of new products or services, improvements (increased productivity) of existing products or services, and reduced cost of production. It is a complex and ever changing mix. What we have is an index of productivity, of the relation between the cost of production and the value of output. What is the rate of productivity gain of the country's leading in scientific and technological development? For the

United States, the productivity growth rate per hour of work has averaged around 2% a year since 1987, about the same as in the previous thirty years.

This index significantly overstates the actual gains. Over time labor has been a decreasing share of the costs of production, capital in particular has been increasing. When productivity trends are calculated on the basis of total factors, not just labor, the annual rate drops to one percent. Even that may overstate gains in recent decades, since they reflect the cost savings from outsourcing production to low-wage countries. The consumption of new products and services that contribute to consumer wellbeing but not to economic output may be at the expense of reduced consumption of other goods and services that do contribute to economic productivity.

It does not take much of an upward trend in costs of production resources or in dependency ratio to counteract growth in productivity in advanced nations. If the rapid growth of China, India and other nations is not to reduce standards of living in affluent nations, the rate of productivity growth must become a multiple of what it has been. The Industrial Revolution has reduced the costs of agriculture and manufacturing to a small fraction of their pre-industrial level. What is left are services. The three largest service industries are government. health care, and education.

The revolution in information, communication and surveillance of the past century will continue. There will be further outsourcing of knowledge from human minds to computers and other electronic devices, outsourcing of functions from human hands and senses to robots. It is a matter of momentum,, but also a response to a declining labor force. Many human workers will become superfluous. Individual self-identification will have to be reinvented for many if not most as traditional jobs and occupations disappear. The hybrid human-computer keyboard is a species of idiot-savant.

What about renewable resources? Hunting and gathering were replaced by animal husbandry and farming, craftsmanship by the factory system. Can we replace natural forests with tree plantations and multiply their productivity? Not much can be done about sustainable fisheries, other than avoiding polluting the marine environment in which they live. There is not enough agricultural land in the planet to produce an American diet for 7 billion people even with the most advanced technology available, and efforts to do so simply involve sacrificing other uses of the land and resources. To feed adequately the 9 billion in mid-century, most of us should become vegetarians. With best agro-technology, best practice yes. But best practice everywhere all the time? Every farmer an agronomist? The prospects of 7 billion humans, 9 billion by mid-century, reducing their footprint on planet resources and environment to sustainable levels is the opium of the classes.

If every other adult owned a car, if every family lived in housing with central heating and air conditioning appropriate to its climate, where would the energy come from? Partly from renewable sources, but still mainly from hydrocarbons or nuclear. Progress on short term storage of energy should allow us to obtain fully one third of our energy needs from intermittent sources by the end of the century.

What many nations are doing is two-pronged: the first prong is substitution of renewable resources for nonrenewable resources, recyclable for non-recyclable resources. Their supply is not sufficient to meet the needs of the developing plus the developed world. The second prong is economy, efficiency in the production and use of scarce and/or depleting resources. We can increase the steady-state output of renewables. Reforestation or tree farming should be practiced instead of simple clear-cutting, just as fish farming is supplementing ocean fisheries, or in the past animal husbandry replaced hunting, farming replaced gathering.

The largest potential gains require social as well as technical change. They involve changing behavior to reduce the demand and need for limited resources. The worst offender in terms of energy use may be the single-family detached house. It is responsible for excessive use of cars and consumption of energy, among other sins. But changing housing patterns is a slow process. Households, business, and government are economizing on communication, transportation and travel as well as office space by relying on the internet. Later this century they will reduce the need for classrooms and doctors' offices as well.

Large increases in demand will soon taper off as rapid growth of underdeveloped nations slows down. But accelerated depletion of non-reproducible resources is not reversible, and overuse of reproducible resources may take generations to counteract. Yes, science and technology have performed miracles, but they are still searching for fusion power and a vaccine for malaria.

The environmental movement is a different subject, by coincidence with the same consequences as overpopulation and resource depletion. Both increase the cost of energy and food products. Greens accentuate these trends by promoting high cost energy and agriculture on an indefinitely continuing basis. Its negative effect on productivity is concentrated in affluent nations. What distinguishes it is its reversal of the relation between \research, invention, and investment. It promotes high cost investment in the expectation that research results will follow and costs fall. It commits resources to technologies it hopes to render obsolete. By subsidizing investment then subsidizing inefficient production it reduces growth. There is no end in sight to this well-intentioned mission. But the long run future of energy is nuclear fission, perhaps fusion, until such time as large scale long term storage of solar energy becomes possible and competitive.

The innovation/imitation ratio, or leader/laggard relation, is reversed when innovation is cost-increasing, choice-reducing. The laggard is able to prolong growth in living levels, or defer decline longer than the leader. The decline will be smaller the longer the delay because over time the cost differences between new and old technologies will lessen. (The reverse of what innovation has been in the past.)

The current concentration is on energy, solar and wind in particular, which are and will remain much more expensive than coal or gas, is counter-productive. Since there is an abundant supply of coal and of natural gas into the 22nd century, the rationale is not exhaustion of stock or cost of supply, but environment. The justification is that carbon dioxide drives climate, that ideal climate is known to be cooler than today's, and that we can change climate at a cost less than the benefit. The first assumption is partially correct, the other two are false. An alternative initial assumption is that population drives climate, and birth control technology is more important than reducing per capita human emissions of carbon dioxide.

A change in priorities is not in sight. Concern for the environment is mandatory. But as the secular religion of the 21st century, its followers count no costs or benefits. Virtuous behavior is its own reward. When Descartes said "Cogito, ergo sum", he was speaking for himself. For most of us, it is "Credo, ergo sum".

As to demographic problems, technology has little further to contribute. It has already accomplished the purpose of reducing fertility in most of the world. What is needed in some nations is information and motivation. Medical research should focus on a rapid reduction in the proportion of the population that spends months and years in nursing homes at the end of their lives. This will not reduce the dependency ratio perhaps, but it will significantly lower its burden on workers. Winning the war on cancer increases longevity, a desideratum that is also a problem.

War and Peace

If the future of fertility is a big unknown, the future of democracy is another, which may tilt the balance between peace and war on a trans-continental scale. In particular, can China make the transition from millennia of despotism, conquest and imperialism to representative government, which its neighbors have succeeded in achieving, or must there be war and fears of war? Democracy is only one aspect of what we consider human rights. These are ecumenical, transcending race, ethnicity, and in particular, nationalism. Racial and ethnic animosity may persist, but it is nationalism in the absence of human rights that threatens the future of mankind.

Conclusion

In sum, the rapid growth of large underdeveloped nations seeking to attain first world living levels will raise the cost and price of resources by accelerating depletion of non-reproducible resources and exceeding consumption at sustainable yield levels of reproducible resources. In most first world nations, this trend will be magnified by a combination of the passing of the large baby boom generation and a decline in birth rates below replacement level, increasing the dependency ratio. The ratio of workers to population will decline as long as successive generations are smaller than their predecessors. Population growth will end, to be followed by decline.

Real wages and levels of living will decline in most advanced nations. Efforts of most large underdeveloped nations to attain first world standards will fail. Resource constraints and rising costs will limit affluence to a minority of world population. Economic growth will become a negative sum game, which can be rendered zero or positive only by technological breakthroughs that cannot be predicted and are highly unlikely in the 21st century.

The world as a whole is overpopulated. Eurasia is overpopulated. So is much of Africa already; soon all of Africa, given current high fertility rates. Advanced nations have no obligation to help nations with fertility rates of 4 and 5 per woman, and may lack the resources. Fertility must fall first. Economic development of billions of people living in the third world is not in the interest of people living in the first world at anything approaching current population levels. Development is a means of reducing population growth, but it is too late. It would have been much better had development succeeded a century earlier, when world population was some 2 billion, compatible with preservation of the stocks of renewable resources. Frustrated aspirations make for a dangerous century.

It is the Americas, not Asia, that can attain and maintain affluence. The hemisphere is not overpopulated; the fertility rate for nearly all its population is at or slightly below replacement level. Dependency ratios will not rise as fast or as far as in Eurasia. It has not had a war in 70 years, a minor one at that. The ratio of resources to population is high. The hemisphere will be a net exporter of resources and a net destination of immigrants. It can benefit during this century from a rising price for agricultural and mineral resources. The Americas are also the ultimate prize for the resource-hungry. The century ahead is a dangerous one.

Hegel once warned us that the tragedy of life was not the conflict between right and wrong, but between right and right. We have too many rights. A pessimist might add that the comedy of life is the conflict between wrong and wrong. Ethics is the choice of the lesser evil; wisdom is the ability to criminate between evils. It is a lesson our descendants must learn if democracy is to survive the century.